Grow Old and

Be Happy

A Work In Progress

By

Michael Rice, LISAC, CTRTC

Grow Old and Be Happy

A Work in Progress

By

Michael Rice, LISAC, CTRTC

Copyright 2016 by Madeira Publishing Company

Madeira Publishing Company
1550 E. University Dr, Suite J-1
Mesa, AZ 85203
480 898-3015
http://www.mike-rice.com

Editor: Lynn Zacny Busby

Artwork by Rob Tong

ISBN-13: 978-1532927508

ISBN-10: 1532927509

Website: http://www.mike-rice.com/

Blog: http://blog.mike-rice.com

Other Books by Michael Rice

	*A Choice Theory Approach to Drug and Alcohol Abuse* ISBN: 1449501079 For addicts/alcoholics, therapists/counselors, and anyone who lives with or loves an addicted person.
	*'Til Death Do Us Part, or 'Til You Piss Me Off, Whichever Comes First* - ISBN: 1449503160 Why marriages and relationships fail and how to put them back together.
	*Happiness is Just a Bowl of Choices* ISBN: 1449500897 Why people do the things they do which destroy what they want the most in life: Happiness. Learn ways to find and keep it.

Choice Theory with Addicted Populations

ISBN: 146094979X

A Diverse Approach for the Treatment of Addictions. This book contains techniques, directives, ideas, and explanations for those who may be addicted to prescription meds, street drugs or alcohol

Leave Me Alone!

ISBN: 1497531861

Direct, blunt, and to the point designed for the reader to see the reality and truth of addiction. Directions and concepts are passed along to the reader to assist them on the road to a drug/alcohol-free life and new-found happiness.

Table of Contents

Dedication To Dr. Ken Larsen

Most people have experienced a close friendship with someone in their life . . . someone who is more than just a friend or an associate . . . but someone with whom you have a very special, close, platonic relationship. If you are really fortunate, you have experienced more than one or two relationships as I describe.

Such is the case of the friendship that I had with Dr. Ken Larsen and to whom I dedicate this book. I met Ken in 2012 by way of our common association with the William Glasser Institute. Ken lived in Apple Valley, MN and I live in Mesa, AZ. I was immediately impressed with Ken's apparent knowledge of many interesting topics. He was interested in my background of music and performing before I had changed careers and became a counselor, as well as my clinical use of Reality Therapy and Choice Theory. We were both raised in parochial schools and had served in the Army at the same time, only in different parts of the world.

Our initial friendship had its occasional disagreements that twice came close to terminating. Those disagreements were usually political in nature or our differences in approaching psychology. Ken, being medically trained, had that medical mind-set towards looking at maladies and mental health. I, on the other hand, am a purist of Dr. Glasser's Choice Theory and knowing that there is no physical pathology to what is being called "mental illness," I stood firm on seeing that the cause of all long term emotional problems are relationship problems that have no medical or physical causes. Ken seemed to want to dig into the human brain to find the causes of what is being called "mental illness." He and I would argue our differences in civil ways and avoid criticizing or trying to change each other. Ken loved a good argument/discussion as long as it was civil. Over the years, we came to meet on middle ground on our differences. In fact, he even began to sway his political preferences during these current election preliminaries. I kidded him by saying, "Come over from the dark side." Once, in a somewhat temperature rising discussion I said, "You know Ken? I could easily take your side on this matter. But then we would both be wrong." We both laughed and put the discussion away respecting each other's points of view.

Our friendship grew over the next couple of years to the point that Ken didn't have to respond to any length to my daily emails of small talk or using him to vent my frustration when dealing with certain clients. He could respond in a very short sentence, or just one word and it would speak volumes to me. He was also the most versed and knowledgeable about the Christian religion than anyone I have ever known. I once asked him why he never pursued the priesthood. He said, "Because they can't marry and have kids." He would sometimes include, in his emails, chapters and verses from the Bible that were applicable to many different situations or concerns going on in my life at the time. I often accused him of having a list of these chapters and verses right next to his computer for cross-reference for any life's situation (which of course he would deny). He actually had them memorized. I would tell him that his thirst for knowledge was due to "that must be the Jesuit in you." On his short one or two word responses to some of my lengthy missives, I jokingly accused him of being too verbose and to please keep his responses short.

In all the years I knew Ken, he never once had anything bad to say about another person even if he didn't care for them. Only rarely would he use the words "damn" or "hell" in a sentence, written or oral. We communicated daily for years either by email or Skype. At least once a year we met for three days a year during our annual Board of Directors meetings or a national conference for the Wm Glasser Institute. We worked together as a team on our writing submissions to Mental Health and Happiness. . . editing and suggesting modifications or additions to our works. We were each other's sounding board. We aired our concerns and discussed many things of which we shared interests.

Ken died in his sleep on February 23, 2016 just ten days after meeting with him at our annual William Glasser Institute - US Board meeting in Dallas, TX. I was absolutely stunned when I received the news and felt a part of me had died as well. He was the finest man I have ever known. To this day, I still feel compelled to send my daily email to him or to receive one from him. He made friends with many people all over the world by way of the William Glasser Institute and was highly respected by all. A classier act you will never find.

Dr. Kenneth Larsen
October 25, 1939 - February 23, 2016

Foreword

On August 23, 2013, William Glasser International lost its leader and mentor, Dr. William Glasser. For the past 50 years, over 90,000 individuals in 43 different countries were trained in Dr. Glasser's concepts of Choice Theory psychology and its applications to counseling (Reality Therapy,) to schools (Glasser Quality Schools,) and to management (Lead Management.) Dr. Glasser's death came as a shock to many of his followers. Even though he was a man of small stature, he was bigger than life to those who came to know him. To say his ideas were ahead of his time is a major understatement, indeed. When you have had the opportunity to learn from a true genius, you tend to think they are indestructible and will live forever. But alas, even geniuses have an expiration date so his followers and William Glasser International went into mourning.

Following Dr. Glasser's death, many others made their transitions as well. Some notable individuals are Linda Harshman, Fitz-George Peters, Barbara Hammel-Olsen, Ray Harris, Bill Abbott, Leon Lojk and most recently, Ken Larsen. All of these individuals had made significant contributions in furthering the work of the

William Glasser Institute and to lose so many in such a short period of time was truly shocking.

Many of the conversations happening in and around the Institute in the past few years were about the future of the Institute. Who will lead us from here? How do we go on with so many gone? How will we handle our grief? And how do we deal with our own mortality? With so many people dying around us, it become difficult not to wonder, *when will it happen to me?*

Mike Rice, in this book, takes an honest, sometimes humorous look, at the aging process, grief and mortality from a Choice Theory point of view. Dr. Glasser taught all of us the importance of relationships in our lives. Every one of us practicing Choice Theory is an expert at creating and maintaining quality relationships in our lives. We all know how important relationships are to our overall mental health and wellbeing. We don't settle for the superficial, but dive deep to connect on a soul level with those important to us. We have learned the lesson of becoming a need satisfying individual to others and how to connect without attempting to externally control others. But somehow we seem to have missed the lesson on how to cope with the loss of these important relationships.

Mike shows us that we have had the tools all along to move forward and reminds us of how to grow old gracefully with the application of Choice Theory psychology. After all, everything we do is a choice. Of course, we don't always get to choose the things that happen to us, but we can always choose our responses to them.

Growing older is inevitable; being depressed or angry is a choice. Loved ones dying is out of our control, but what we focus on – the pain of loss or the power of the relationship – is our choice. Our body's eventual decline, if we are privileged to live that long, is a natural part of the life cycle, but whether we focus on the things we *can't* do anymore or the gratitude for what we *can* is our choice.

Mike expertly helps us see these truths and face our future with courage, hope, gratitude and a wonderful sense of humor.

Kim Olver, Executive Director
William Glasser International
and William Glasser Institute – US

Wisdom That Comes From Age

Remember when we were kids? Time seemed to go on forever. A week was like a year. A year was like an eternity. We did so many things in one day when we were kids that time seemed to stand still. Then we got older and began to gradually slow down with each passing year. As we slowed down, time appeared to speed up.

I can vividly recall being forty years old and the next thing I knew I was 70. What the hell happened? I'm reminded of the verse to a Frank Sinatra song, "One day you turn around, and it's summer. Next day you turn around, and it's fall. And all the springs and winters of a lifetime . . . whatever happened to them all." And then there's that line from another Sinatra song: "Last night, when we were young . . .. Ages Ago . . .. Last Night."

I look back on my life's years with many, many memories . . . some very sad and some very happy. I'm grateful for every one of them. I look back on the things I've accomplished and those at which I failed, the wonderful relationships, both romantic and platonic,

14

and the not so wonderful relationships. I've accomplished more than I give myself credit for doing. I've learned, and lived, cried, and laughed through life and these are the things that make us who we are. Oh the stories we all could tell.

I have taken the opportunity to put many of my thoughts into words and share with you what I have learned that guide my travels through the September of my years. The roadmap given me on this journey comes from everyone I have ever met. They have become a part of me. I pay special tribute to those whom I have known who have gone before me.

Give thanks for every day you wake up. It sure beats the alternative. Just because you are older doesn't mean you have to stop accomplishing anything each day. Continue to dream and create. Live and love.

Most of all of my friends have been older than I. I have this desire to learn from those older than myself and gain some insight and wisdom from all of their knowledge and life's experiences.

I always respected my elders. Now that I'm their age, I don't have to respect anyone.

I used to joke by saying, "If you want to look young . . . hang out with old people." I thought this was a clever line until one day, all of my older friends were no longer living and I became the old one.

I had learned from every one of them, including how they dealt with illness, suffering, and finally . . . their death. I am a part of each and every one of them. Here are some of the things they taught me from their experiences and acquired wisdom:

- You don't have to be right all of the time.
- You don't have to agree with everyone all of the time.
- Learn to discuss your differences with civility and respect and honor the rights of others to believe whatever they believe without you trying to change them.
- Any major differences you may have with someone close is best avoided rather than getting into heated discussions about your differences. Live and let live.
- You don't have to live up to anyone's standards but your own.

- If someone doesn't like you, you aren't the one with the problem.
- You have the right to say "No."
- What is right for you does not make it right for everyone else.
- Mind your own business the way you want to and let others mind their own business the way they want to.
- Criticizing, blaming, complaining, nagging, threatening, punishing, and bribing others will only distance you from people . . . especially those who are important to you.
- In Business: Your friends don't make you money.
- No one becomes successful without the help of others.
- In relationships/marriage: When there is conflict, focus on the importance of that marriage or relationship more than the issue in which you disagree or have conflict. Think before you act. Will what you are about to say or do bring you closer to that person or will it drive you further apart?
- Be punctual in appointments. It shows respect and begets respect from others.

- Be responsible for all of your obligations. Don't procrastinate on any of your responsibilities. Do them so you don't have to fret about them until you get around to them. Holding off from responsibilities will only create stress and unhappiness.
- You can't drink or drug your problems away.
- You and only you are responsible for your own happiness so don't expect it to come from others.
- Ask for help when you need it. Asking is a sign of strength, not weakness.
- Admit when you're wrong.
- Apologize and make amends when necessary. We all make mistakes. (Not everyone has to accept your apologies).
- Be grateful for all the things you have accomplished and acquired and have faith that you will continue to be blessed.
- Expand your knowledge. Just because you may have completed your scholastic education does not mean that you have learned all you need to know . . . not by a long shot. Life and death have a lot to teach all of us far more than our schooling. Read, research, and observe as

18

much as you can about the things that are important in life.

- Distance yourself from toxic people (even if they are family members).
- Don't dwell in the past over any unjust or hurtful actions of others (both real and imagined). It keeps you stuck in the role of a victim and keeps you from happiness and moving on.
- Forgive yourself for any and all of your own past actions that may have harmed others as well as yourself. We're humans. We often screw up.
- Slow down. Life doesn't have to be an everlasting race to the finish.
- Acquire meaningful relationships. The more you have, the happier you will be.

These are just some of the things that I have learned from life and from my friends. Academia doesn't teach you these things. I'm sure that many of you have heard or read many of these platitudes before. They don't seem to ever sink in until we reach an older age. As we age, we tend to look back and recall them and suddenly have an epiphany. . . "Oh, now I get it."

What if you knew that you only had so much time left before you would die? What would you do? Some have made a bucket list of the things they would like to do before they die or "kick the bucket." Others have prepared for their final day by making a will that contains instructions on what to do when their time comes and how to distribute their assets. Most people, it seems, put dying out of their mind and rarely, if ever, think about it . . . preferring to think only in the now (and often the past) . . . denying that day will come until reality sets in and denial is no longer an option.

There are 4 things we cannot control:

- The weather
- The past
- Growing older
- Living forever

Some of you may be inclined to say that we can control other people and that would be true to some extent. We cannot easily control another person without harming the relationship with that person.

Weather happens. It's all part of the nature of our planet.

The past is just that . . . the past. Whatever has happened in the past cannot be changed: good, bad, or indifferent. While it may have a part in your development, it has very little to do with finding happiness that you want today and tomorrow.

Growing older is inevitable. The body ages more than the mind in most cases. In nature, nothing lasts forever. Everything changes.

Death will eventually come to all of us at some time or another. This too, is a fact of the life cycle of all living things. So the truth is: We actually do only have so much time to live.

Today, we are living longer than those who were born in much earlier generations. Medicines can and do save lives but they rarely cure any illness that is not of an infectious nature. While life is extended, the quality of life does not always go hand in hand with the extension. And this will be main area of subject matter in this book: Dealing with aging and death . . . of our loved ones and ourselves. I believe it was Lawrence Taylor who once asked Walter Payton, who was dying of liver disease, "Are you scared?" Walter replied, "Yes, 'cause I've never died before."

While it is true, we don't have the experience of having died before, we have, most likely, seen prior deaths of family and friends. It is these experiences that we tend to recall when thinking of our own impending death. Dying is a scary thought. After all . . . none of us have done it before and there is something about the unknown that adds anxiety and fear. In all of my experiences of those who have died and those who have discussed dying, those who possessed a strong religious belief in the afterlife seemed to deal with it better than those who didn't share this belief. Faith can play a very important role in our lives. Many fallen-away Christians have found their way back when knowing their life is coming to an end.

There are many ways to die but we all hope that when our time comes, it is not a painful, long, drawn-out process.

The potential lifespan of men and women are more similar now than at any time since the early 1950s, when the life expectancy of women was just over 70, and men could expect to live only to their late 60s[1]. Generally, women lived 7 years longer than men back then. Today, that gap has narrowed. Those born in the 1980s will find that women live only 4 years longer than men.

On a personal basis, I have known several friends and family members who have died, as I am fairly sure you have experienced as well. It wasn't until my later years that I took dying seriously enough to note how those who were dying were dealing with their impending death.

Some were fearful as they had lived their life denying the day would come. Others had no choice to think or prepare for it and died unexpectedly. Then there were those who put up a courageous front yet feared and worried about what would happen to those they loved after their death. Finally, there were those who knew they were dying, accepted it, and continued to live as if nothing was happening until they physically got to the point of incapacitation.

---

[1] Doughty, Steve. (2013 October 24). Daily Mail. Retrieved from http://www.dailymail.co.uk/news/article-2474859/Life-expectancy-gap-men-women-narrows-years.html#ixzz479vHoNWU

My first experience with death was with my maternal grandparents. I was not particularly close to them so their deaths had minimal effect on me other than to think how sad that they are now no longer on this earth.

Irene

My next experience with death was one of tremendous awareness of the Christian/Judeo concept of body and soul. I had been invited by an associate to attend an anatomy class at a well-known chiropractic college in St. Louis. The classroom was similar in size to a basketball court. There were 12 or so gurneys upon which rested the sheet-covered remains of unclaimed bodies and those whose bodies who had been donated to science.

The students wore white scrubs, gloves, and masks to protect their own clothing from possibly coming in direct contact with the deceased. I was given the same type of clothing to cover myself as well. While I felt a sense of reverence and respect for those who had died, I was appalled to see that some of the students had things written on the back of their scrubs such as, "Manny's Meat Market," and "Joe's Butcher Shop." Some were casually leaning on the bodies as if they were leaning on a desktop, waiting for the class to begin. When I saw this and other things that I won't disclose in order to save you the image, I was appalled at what I was witnessing and that here were students being disrespectful of the dead.

The sheet was removed from the cadaver from which my associate and I and five of his fellow classmates would learn. My attendance made it seven of us surrounding the body. It was a small, slender African American woman whose body tag stated she was 90 years of age when she died and her name was Irene. All of her internal organs had been removed and she had an open body cavity. You can imagine the effect this experience was having on this young 23 year-old, naïve young man's emotions. I was both shocked and curious. I even felt that I was possibly doing wrong by even being there.

The instructing doctor then arrived and began to ask the students to find a particular nerve in the sole of the foot. The students took their scalpels and began cutting into Irene's foot looking for the thinner than thread nerve that was pictured in the text book. I became intently involved watching them seek the nerve while I was on the lookout for it as well. They took turns seeking the nerve and one of the students said to me, "Here, you have a go at it." By now, I was so intent on finding that nerve that I automatically took the scalpel and began cutting through Irene's flesh and found it.

I was so proud that I had accomplished the deed that I then turned the scalpel to yet another student who would seek the nerve in Irene's other foot. I was so involved that I suddenly became shocked when I realized that I was now casually leaning on Irene's body while watching the other students seek the elusive thin nerve.

It was at this moment that I suddenly became aware of something that was so awesome in nature that it would stay with me all through my waking hours of the day for over a week. And this is what I came to realize: As complicated as the human body is, (it is truly a miraculous creation) the human body is no more than a shell . . . a way for us to move about, express ourselves, and complete tasks . . . that the body that lay before me was no longer Irene, and that it never was. Irene was a soul that was contained in her brain and her being. Her body and soul and spirit were no longer one and the same. Irene was gone. Only her shell remained.

A gush of air exited my lungs and I went into a staring gaze from which I found difficult to recover. Eight years of parochial school at St. Bernard's and hearing about "the soul" finally made absolute sense to me. I now realized what the nuns had been talking about that had previously been an intangible and invisible subject and no more than empty rhetoric at the time. I gasped again. In fact, I gasped for several days afterwards.

Irene had taught me one of the most important lessons of my life. I began to see others differently . . .based on their words, behavior, and knowledge (or lack of) rather than how they looked physically. I began to see myself differently as well, realizing that my physical appearance was not who I really was. Irene's death brought new meaning to my life and that of others.

To this day, I become sad and discouraged when I hear people criticizing and labeling others based on their physical appearance or behavior. Those who do so are not happy people and don't even like themselves. They have yet to learn, if ever, that the soul is separate from the body. We are not our behavior. We are people who behave. And all of our behavior is chosen to satisfy happiness, pleasure, or both.

> The bitter, yet merciful, lesson which death teaches us is to distinguish the gold from the tinsel, the true values from the worthless chaff. The terrible events of life are great eye-openers. They force us to learn that which it is wholesome for us to know, but which habitually we try to ignore — namely, that really we have no claim on a long life; that we are each of us liable to be called off at any moment, and that the main point is not how long we live, but with what meaning we fill the short allotted span — for short it is at best.[2]

Death is the end of life of a biological organism. On a lighter note: Robin Williams told us, " Death is nature's way of saying, "Your table's ready." The life cycle exists in all living organisms. Life is the result of cells that continuously die and regenerate and wear themselves out in the process. Metabolism slows down

---

[2]Felix Adler, *Life and Destiny* (1913), Section 8: Suffering and Consolation

and cells begin to die and not regenerate as well as they used to. This leads to any number of complications the body can experience. Name an illness and you are identifying either an infection or cellular malfunctioning.

The most common ways people express their unhappiness is through aches and pains. Conversely, aches and pains commonly cause unhappiness. Not only do we have a separation of body and soul, we also have a distinct separation yet strong connection with that of the mind and the physical body. The mind is capable of creating unhappy thoughts that are stressful to body organs and cellular structure.

Fibromyalgia

One of the most common conditions today is something that is being called, Fibromyalgia. This is a painful condition for which no physical cause seems to exist. The pain is real. It isn't imagined. Yet there is no direct physical cause for the pain. There are many doctors who will prescribe addictive opiate pain medications and other doctors who don't prescribe anything. Further information on Fibromyalgia can be attained from Dr. William Glasser's book, "Fibromyalgia: Hope from a Completely New Perspective." [3]

I have had several women as clients who had been told they were suffering from Fibromyalgia. In every case, it was a client who was going through an unhappy divorce at the time. It seems that those who report suffering from Fibromyalgia tend to primarily be female and going through some very unhappy times. I have not, as yet, had a male client report that he suffers from Fibromyalgia. This is not to say men don't suffer from it. They are more inclined to deny they are having any difficulty in their relationships even when the relationship is headed towards the rocks.

A few years ago, a classmate of mine who attended that same Parochial school I spoke about earlier, as well as high school, connected with me after some fifty years. She, being two years older, had graduated high school before I did. We lost touch with each other after that. By way of the Internet, we found each other again. She began to email me telling me about her life since we last attended school together. She had

---

[3]Retrieved from http://www.amazon.co.uk/Fibromyalgia-Glassier-W/dp/0967844428

married and had two sons. Her husband died of lung cancer only a few years ago.

In one of her emails, she wrote me and said she was suffering from a sudden onset of pain in her right shoulder. She asked if I thought she should see a doctor. I informed her that I was not a medical practitioner so I couldn't really advise her on that matter but that if she felt the need to do so, then she should see her doctor. Being a therapist, I did ask her a question that comes automatically to me when I hear someone tell me they are suffering from general aches and pains. I asked her, "Is there any important person in your life that you are having difficulty with?" She denied any such situation. So I rephrased the question: "Is there someone important to you that you are not satisfied with the relationship you currently have with them?" Again, she denied such a scenario.

My next question to her was, "How long ago did this pain begin?" She replied, "Two days ago." I asked, "What were you doing or what were you thinking about for the better part of the day two days ago?" After a long period of thought she answered, "I was thinking that in the next few days, it would be the anniversary of

31

my husband's death." It so happened that the next day was the anniversary date she spoke of. I then said, "If the pain is not unbearable and something you can live with for the next couple of days, then you may not wish to see a doctor. That's up to you. But if it is unbearable, then I would advise you see your doctor." Three days later, and two days after the anniversary of her husband's death, she reported that the pain was gone and no longer a problem.

Who in her life was behaving in a way in which she disapproved? She disapproved of her husband's death and wanted him to still be a part of her life. Thinking about her loss and not having the relationship they had shared for many years tended to enhance her unhappiness and lead to her physical pain. Her husband had been the only man she had ever dated or married and was a major part of her life.

Total Behavior

This might be a good place for me to explain to you something that is called, "Total Behavior." The Total Behavior concept was created and explained by Dr. William Glasser, MD, a Board Certified psychiatrist known all over the world.

The common definition of behavior is, "The manner in which one acts or behaves." Dr. Glasser explains that behavior is the result of four separate functions. He calls these four components, "Total Behavior." The four components of behavior are

1. Thinking
2. Acting
3. Physiology and
4. Emotions.

First we think. Each thought consists of an emotion of happy, unhappy, or neutral. It is impossible to have an emotion without a preceded thought. If you are angry, you are thinking unwanted, angry, or fearful thoughts. If you are happy, you are thinking of happy or pleasurable thoughts. If you have no positive or negative emotions, your thoughts are neutral or indifferent and not affecting your emotions.

There is nothing in the world that can make you unhappy other than your own thoughts about what you perceive.

With each positive or negative emotion, something within your body will respond in positive or negative ways. You've heard that laughter is the best medicine. There is a lot to be said for that. Unhappy thoughts cause internal stress on different parts of the body including internal organs. Wherever one may have a weakened condition, negative and unhappy thoughts tend to exacerbate the condition.

The last of the four components of Total Behavior is Acting. Acting is the manner in which we behave to express our unhappiness as well as behaviors designed to alleviate unhappiness in some way or another or to cause happiness or pleasure. Acting is a choice that is made based upon previously learned ways to express one's self, achieve happiness or pleasure, or ease frustration from unwanted situations. If there are no prior experiences one can refer to in the past to relieve this unhappiness, it is very common for individuals to create a behavior that is designed to purposefully achieve happiness or pleasure, or both. All we do from birth until death is behave and most all behavior is a choice that is designed to relieve unhappiness or to add pleasure. These creative or previously used choices can be either effective or maladaptive and will show themselves throughout this book on aging and death. I will refer back to Total Behavior and how it affects our attitude and subsequent behaviors relating to the aging process in later chapters.

Entering Geezerhood

Bette Davis is famous for having said, "Growing old ain't for sissies" and I must agree.

The difficult thing about aging is that our minds still think we're younger than we are until our body reminds us otherwise. We are reminded when the things we used to do with relative ease can no longer be completed without joint pains in the shoulders and knees as well as not being able to see well enough to do the job. Eyesight now begins to get progressively worse. We begin to require glasses or contacts and eventually, cataracts may develop and for some . . . macular degeneration or glaucoma.

Hair begins to thin and turn gray or white. What you used to groom daily on your head is now going down the drain and some of it is now taking root in your ears, nostrils, and even on your shoulders. You may even notice your ears and nose are beginning to enlarge.

Cells that support the layers of skin begin to break down and wrinkles develop facially and perhaps on your knees as well. Women tend to get wrinkle lines around their mouths. Natural body oil begins to dry up causing dry skin.

Things called skin tags and other barnacles begin to grow on our body. Patches of skin may discolor and brown spots emerge on the back of hands and on arms.

Short-term memory lapses increase over time. You may think of something you want to do and by the time you get out of your chair to do it, you have forgotten what it was you were going to do. They say that three things begin to fade with the onset of aging. One is your short-term memory and I can't remember the other two.

You may be talking with someone and while you know what it is that you want to say, you forget what it is that you wanted to say when it is your turn to speak. You may find that you can't remember certain words that you wanted to use. At first you may find this annoying and frustrating but it does have a positive benefit: You will start to stop worrying about forgetting because you'll forget the things you forgot.

It's important to point out that not everyone who ages will experience all of these things. I have known people in their 80s and 90s who had excellent memory. Mark Twain said, "When I was younger, I could remember anything, whether it happened or not."

Insomnia and mood swings are common. Tolerances to little annoyances shorten and you may find yourself getting upset more often over minor or unimportant issues that never used to bother you. You start to cringe when you have to sneeze or cough for fear of what may come out the other end.

Hearing begins to diminish and words that have consonants are not clearly understood. Tinnitus buzzes or rings all day in the ears to the point of madness. Hearing aids become a standard part of things you wear. You find yourself saying, "What?" many times when talking to others. You smile a lot more and nod your head seriously hoping that what you are responding to was a question that required an agreement.

Gum disease and loss of teeth introduce us to partials and even complete sets of false teeth. 75% of adults over the age of 35 will get gum disease. An alarming 42% of people over 65 are totally toothless.[4]

You know you're getting old when you sink your teeth into a hamburger and they stay there.

The spongy cartilage protecting our joints to absorb shock and add spring to our step wears out. Joints ache and muscle strength wanes. Also, loss of height by as much as 2 inches may occur due to loss of fluid in vertebrae and causing them to compress.

---

[4]Retrieved from www.psychologytoday.com/articles/199311/how-the-body-ages

Osteoporosis is common in women. Varicose veins emerge. Skin dries up and starts to look like crepe paper. Muscle mass begins to deflate by as much as 23% between 30 and 70 years of age. (Exercise prevents and/or slows it down). Jowls develop and double chins appear. Gravity is taking over. The body begins to spread in places you didn't know were possible. Your knees buckle but your belt doesn't. Getting out of the car is not as easy as it used to be. Tasks that require bending over or kneeling such as gardening, will now require something to hold onto for support in order to pull yourself back up to a standing position.

You think all your friends are starting to look older but you don't think you do. Your feet become tender and stepping on something as small as a grain of rice feels like you stepped on a large sharp stone. Plantar fasciitis comes from shrinking tendons in the soles of the feet. In the morning you walk in short, tender, painful steps until you stretch the tendons back out. One or both of your hips begin to hurt after walking longer than you normally do. This is bone rubbing against bone and/or tendonitis.

Between the ages of 20 to 70, lung capacity can decrease by almost 40%. If a past smoker, your lung capacity is far from what it used to be even when you were a smoker. You could lose up to 80% of your lung capacity to breathe. If a current smoker, you will have several other complications besides loss of breath and COPD. Sleep apnea is a common condition requiring a CPAP machine to keep you breathing during sleep.

Women will begin to have hot flashes. Men will begin to have prostate problems and perhaps Erectile Dysfunction (ED). Urination begins to be more frequent and difficult, starting and feeling like you have voided your bladder when you really haven't. I was once asked, "Do you wear boxers or briefs?" I replied, "Depends."

Body fat begins to redistribute under the skin to the waist, thighs, and rear end. Now those slices of cake, bowls of ice cream, and slices of pizza are going directly to those fatty areas. By now, you may even begin to think you are starting to look like a painting by Picasso. These are just some of the most common things that happen to us when we age. You may not experience all of them but you will surely receive a good share of them.

You have to face the reality that you are old when you sit in a rocking chair and can't get it started.

I'm reminded of the effect aging has on salmon that return from the sea to their original fresh water streams where they were hatched. Their long sleek silver bodies begin to turn red, develop long pointed faces with gnarly, protruding teeth, and a large hump develops on their backs. They fertilize the eggs the female releases and then they both die soon afterwards. I can think of worse ways to die but dying after sex can only be surpassed by dying in one's sleep in my opinion. It sure beats getting hit by a bus or dying from cancer.

There are also more serious common conditions such as Heart Disease, Pancreatitis, Kidney problems, Liver problems; cancers of breast, colon, ovaries, lung, brain, skin, and prostate. All of us have the genetics to suffer from such maladies. All men will develop prostate cancer in their lifetime. Many may die of other causes before the prostate cancer does them in. Why some

42

people experience these serious physical ailments and others don't is due primarily to their lifestyle.

Most people die as a result of the things they have been putting in their mouths for years. Some of these things are alcohol, drugs, fatty foods, processed and fast foods, diet drinks, cigarettes and chewing tobacco, sugar, and prescription drugs.

Some of these conditions are unavoidable while others are preventable. A lot of it depends on your diet, the amount of exercise you get, and the bad habits you may have had that you no longer possess. You've heard it thousands of times: The key to good health is **DIET** and **EXERCISE.** There are no other substitutes. **KEEP MOVING**. Avoid becoming stagnant or sedentary. **MOVE.** Even if the only exercise you do is walk, it is better than not doing anything at all.

On a personal note, I took the initiative to start an early morning walk around my neighborhood each morning. At first, I couldn't walk very far without getting out of breath (I am an ex-smoker), and a pain in my left hip. I had attempted this challenge several times before and would always stop the program after two days due to my shortness of breath and hip pain. It's very easy to allow discomfort to override our wants and goals. However on one particular attempt, I convinced myself to walk anyway and to endure the pain. In only 4 days, my hip pain went away and my breathing improved. I eventually was able to increase the distance I was walking from one block to four blocks totaling a mile.

WALK. Walk around your neighborhood in the early morning hours before the sun comes up or evening when the sun has set (depending on the weather). Bundle up if the weather is cold. Avoid walking on ice or in snow. Your ability to keep your balance may not be what it once was. Stay off of ladders no matter how well you think you can use one. Go to the mall and walk all the levels without stopping to do any window shopping until you've walked a good distance. Swimming and bicycling are also great exercises. If you have a Medicare program, there are some programs that cover your use of the larger spas and gyms in your town. I have a program with my health care that is called "Silver Sneakers," that allows me to use the exercise equipment and pool at a major health club at no cost.

Caregivers Beware

A common scenario I have experienced in my counseling is that of the person who becomes a caregiver to a loved one. They begin to do things for their loved one that the loved one could do for themselves. My mother was this type of a person. When my father was diagnosed with a congenital heart condition as well as prostate cancer and type II diabetes, she began doing everything for him. The only exercise he got was to get out of bed and sit in his recliner all day to either write or watch TV and then move back to his bed at night. She brought his meals to him on a tray. She brushed his teeth (they were false), she trimmed his toenails, held a urine bottle for him to pee in, combed his hair, and fed him some of the harmful foods that contributed towards his illness. She would justify this by saying, "I give him these foods because he likes them so much." This is an excellent example of loving someone to death.

My father's muscle tone disappeared. He had no strength to even walk and often fell on his way to the bathroom to relieve his bowels and not make it in time. He was 82 when he died. No one lives forever but he could have added several more years to his life had he moved around more and did the things that he could have done for himself. My mother, however . . . a woman who ate minimally and "only to stay alive," exercised regularly by walking a mile once or twice a week. She lived to the age of 96.

Retirement

Men tend to base their identity and self-worth on their occupational duties and skills. Women tend to identify by their marriage and family. However, there are an increasing number of women who are getting married later and also identify with their occupation along with being a caregiver and mother.

Two things are known to happen with men and women who retire and the kids have all grown. With no children to raise, there may be a sense of losing one's purpose to varying degrees. When a man no longer is working, he tends to lose a bit of his worth and identity.

Have you ever noticed how men often tell stories of their past accomplishments and achievements when they get together after retiring? You may even have heard their stories several times. Women tend to have their own social groups after retirement and they tend to be more active than the men and open to doing activities that the husband may not particularly care to do. They talk about their children or grandchildren.

Women also keep in touch with their adult children and grandchildren which allows them to continue the parenting role, although to a lesser degree. Men often enjoy their grandchildren because they feel they may not have been very present with their own children when they were growing up. They may justify their absence by saying that their job required more of their time and effort during those years or that the job was so demanding that they just didn't have the energy and time to devote to being a more attentive, participating fulltime father.

At any rate, when one retires, the idea is to slow down and enjoy life. But after awhile, this new lifestyle may tend to get boring. While some men may be satisfied just to sit around and watch TV, others may take up golf. While some men may be reluctant to go to the mall with their wives, others may join a gym or socialize with other retirees at regular times at a usual place. Some retired couples enjoy traveling while others may prefer to stay at home. Since the wife doesn't want to travel alone, she too begins to stay at home when she would much rather be doing other things or going to other places.

Many women complain that their retired husbands tend to get in the way and interrupt their daily routines. . . trying to convince the wife of a better way of doing things or asking them to justify why they do what they do.

Another very common scenario is how soon a wife dies after her husband dies. With the kids grown and gone, she maintained her identity and purpose in life by caring for her husband. When the husband dies, those who have the strongest identity of tending to the welfare and needs of children and spouse may soon die after the husband dies. I have even noticed this phenomenological aspect with some of my dearest friends.

Ben and Winifred

Two of my closest friends were 23 years my senior (real names not used.) They were retired and refused to live a life of non-activity. They purchased a home in a neighborhood of young married couples with children. They had many friends and I would visit with them for many years in their retirement, often going out to dinner two or three times a month.

Ben was a tall man in stature. His presence was that of a leader. He was a retired Dean of Academic Services and before that, an insurance commissioner for a Midwestern state. He loved to associate with both those in his age group as well as those of us who were younger. In his retirement, he would often "hold court" and talk politics, pontificate, or proclaim his past victories.

Winifred, his wife, was a sweet and thoughtful woman. Both of them came from an era where women and men had a more distinct and expected "duties" to perform in a marriage. In short, if Ben had any shortcomings, he was chauvinistic . . . this being part of his cultural upbringing in their era. Winifred didn't object for she had learned in her own family and generation that this was the role she was expected to play. She did so willingly. She tolerated many controlling behaviors that I considered to be outdated and disrespectful. This was their marriage and they had stayed married for well over 50 years. It was not my place to say anything or to criticize their relationship. It was their generation.

Ben and I became the best of friends. We often played golf or spent many hours playing cards while Winifred would later prepare an excellent pot roast for us. Ben and I used to play Cribbage . . . a card game that Ben had taught me. Ben hated to lose at anything, even if it was parlor game. On the few occasions where this novice cribbage player would beat him at his own game, he would sometimes lose his temper, throw the deck of cards across the room and demand Winifred, "Bring me another deck of cards!" It didn't happen often but it did happen to the point where I finally spoke up and declared that if this is what was to become commonplace whenever he lost the game, then I no longer wished to play the game. His actions were taking the fun out of the game. That's when we began playing Gin Rummy and never again, ever, did we play cribbage.

At the age of 85, Ben was diagnosed with prostate cancer. There was nothing that could be done for him at that time because the cancer had spread too far. Even though he had regular checkups at the Mayo Clinic, either his cancer came on very quickly or it was overlooked at all of his checkups. This is yet another reason for managing your own health which I will cover later.

Ben accepted his impending death and continued to live life as usual much as he had all the years before. We still played cards, went out to dinner, and he continued to work in his yard tending to all of his plants. He never spoke of his impending death or complained about his illness. In fact, he would boast about his weight loss (the result of his illness). Towards the end, he opted for in-home hospice rather than die in a hospital.

Ben remained active and in good spirits up until the last week of his life. His pain became so intense that he was taking opiate pain relievers and became bed ridden. Going out to dinner and our card games were no longer things we would do together. The last few days of his life, I went to visit him. Ben was on the phone talking to all of the people he knew back in the Midwest and with all his past associations. His spirit was uplifting and he wanted to thank everyone for having been a part of his life. There was no sadness or remorse in his voice. His conversations would never lend themselves to sadness or regrets. Occasionally, he would wince in pain but that would be the extent of his suffering that I witnessed.

He looked at me and said, "You've been a good friend." I took his hand and held it and said, "I refuse to say 'goodbye' to you." I held his hand for so long that he began to feel uncomfortable about it and he let go.

Ben was atheistic and yet was not afraid of dying. He accepted the life cycle and dealt with it matter-of-factly, as a natural part of life. Two days after visiting with him, I called to check up on him. His daughter answered the phone and when I asked about him she said, "He just died this very instant as your call came though on the first ring." I ended the conversation knowing that she and her mother had many things they now had to do. Ben taught me how to die with dignity when my time comes. I recall thinking to myself, "This is how I want to leave this life . . . grateful and accepting of the end with no remorse or feeling sorry for myself, and hopefully without suffering."

I maintained contact with Winifred after Ben died. We would go to lunch or she would invite me over for dinner. Several months later, I called to see how she was doing and she reported that she had fallen. She didn't make a big deal out of it. Another month went by and I called to see if she would like to go out for dinner.

She reported having fallen again so she declined the offer. A few short weeks later, her daughter, who lived over 300 miles away, called to tell me that Winifred had died. Winifred had had no physical illness or ailments of which I was aware or of which she had reported. Her cause of death was never disclosed to me.

Winifred had been living alone since Ben died and none of the people that Ben knew, who used to regularly visit, were coming by anymore. Being a seemingly healthy woman of her age, Winifred died soon after the death of her husband. Her life had changed when Ben died to the point that she had lost her role as caregiver and wife. This scenario happens all too often after the death of a spouse. It is not gender-specific although it does appear to happen more often with women than men.

There's an old joke that I recall from several years ago. Why do most men die before their wives die? Because they WANT to. So much for my acceptance and connection with my female readers.

Club Curmudgeon

Have you ever noticed that there are some people who live in retirement or in the September of their years completely upbeat, happy, and active, while others appear to be angry, unhappy, sad, and lonely? What separates these two groups? Why are some happy and others miserable? There are even those who behave as if they are entitled to certain privileges because they have lived so long . . . that now the world owes them.

When older couples, or even older singles, get together, the conversation almost always gravitates to discussing individual health problems, medical conditions, and complaints or experiences concerning their doctors or health care insurance. "Organ recitals" become a regular occurrence with every social gathering.

You might be inclined to respond that unhappy people are unhappy because of some of the following reasons:

- They're angry because they never accomplished all that they wanted to in their life and feel it's now too late.
- They raised kids that caused them nothing but trouble.
- They have a hard time living on their social security and have inadequate finances.
- They're in poor health.
- The wife died or left him alone or the husband died or left her alone.
- All their close friends have died.
- They're subsidizing their kid's lives and family.
- One or more of their kids are still living at home.

- They're still raising kids that belong to their son or daughter.
- They have unresolved issues from the past.
- They fear dying.
- They're alone and lonely.
- They have no interests, detach, and isolate.
- They're bored.
- They drink too much alcohol or are addicted to prescribed medications.

These are all viable causes for one to become angry, irritable, or depressed. However, there are those who are experiencing some or many of the same conditions and are active, happy, positive, outgoing individuals. I believe that many of the elderly become angry out of frustration from not being able to do the things they used to do because of some form of physical impairments that come from aging. Many become "grumpy" because they are living with constant aches and pains every day and night.

I could shorten the above list of why people are unhappy with only two words:

Unsatisfying Relationships

Surely there are other causes of unhappiness such as living in a war-torn area, severe poverty, surviving an earthquake, tsunamis, floods, tornados, or homes destroyed by fire. These are not happy situations by any means. But they are not the primary reasons of why people are seemingly unhappy most of the time.

Let's face it. None of us are happy all of the time. We do experience things from time to time that lead us to choose unhappiness. Even very unhappy people aren't unhappy all of the time either. They do find some occasional happiness.

People are unhappy because they are not having the relationship they would like to have with someone important to them. That someone might also include themselves. Just look, once again, at the above list of reasons that some people use to justify their unhappiness. Each and every one of them has to do with unsatisfying relationships with someone else or even themselves.

Someone is not behaving in the manner that they would like them to behave.

So how is it that some people are unhappy and miserable while others who may be experiencing the same unhappy situations are happy? What is this magic ability that distinguishes them and sets them apart from each other? The answer: **ATTITUDE**.

Where or how does one develop this attitude? The answer: From **PERCEPTION and a CHOICE.** How you perceive things has a direct influence on your attitude: Positive, negative, or neutral. Your perception and attitude have a direct influence on your emotions, physical health, thoughts, and behavior.

Life is a Mental Photo Album

Here's a short, simple explanation of how our brains work: The world is full of pictures. We see them, smell them, taste them, hear them, and feel them through our five senses. We receive these images all day and night. They give us information. Those images that we really like are those that we store in our mental picture album. These images consist of friends, family, our self-image, our values and beliefs, as well as all of those things that are important to us and the way we want things to be or the way we think they "should" be. In short, they are pictures of all those things that contribute to our happiness.

We are constantly receiving information by the pictures we see outside our album. In and of themselves, the pictures outside our album only give us information and information, alone, does not result in behavior. It's what we choose to do with this information that will determine how we react to it. The information is quickly discerned as positive, negative, or perhaps indifferent. Whenever a picture comes into view that does not match the picture we have in our photo album, there tends to be a glitch in one's happiness throwing "something" out of balance. The natural tendency is to say or do something in an attempt to make the pictures match. You know . . . trying to control it.

If you recall, I stated earlier that the cause of most unhappiness is due to unsatisfying relationships . . . someone is behaving in a way in which you disapprove." Therefore, the image that does not match the image in one's photo album will most likely involve something that was said or done, or something that was not said or done, by another person.

How you perceive the difference between what you see and what you want will determine your attitude. If the discrepancy between the images is minor or if it involves someone of little importance to you, your frustration or unhappiness may be only slight and may be quickly forgotten. However, if it involves an issue that you consider of strong importance, or with someone important to you, you may be inclined to react in a negative and even forceful way to make the discrepancy match the image you want.

Not only does the image not match the preferred image of those things that make you happy, but it also depletes other needs, of which you are genetically predisposed, that are designed to *maintain* your happiness and wellbeing.

Here's Why We Behave the Way We Do

The following five topics are things that we strive to satisfy each and every day of our lives. The more each of them is satisfied, the happier we are. We want nothing more than to be happy. These "needs" are the motivation of our behavior and if any one of them is not being satisfied, we become less happy and choose behaviors designed to get their levels to a more satisfying state.[5] There isn't anything that you do that is not intended to satisfy any one or more of these needs. They are genetic in nature and we are all hard-wired to have them to varying degrees. Some people's needs are stronger than those of others. We are all different.

Survival and Safety

The will to survive is strong indeed. When threatened with the loss of survival and/or safety, there is a tendency to become stressed and anxious. We need our health, food, shelter, clothing, and adequate finances to maintain our sense of happiness and wellbeing. There is also

[5]Wm Glasser, 1998, Choice Theory, pp 31-41, Harper Collins, New York, NY

the genetic need for reproduction but at this late stage of life, reproduction is not one of any great importance. Ironically, the behavior that leads to procreation may still be prevalent to varying degrees but not as strong as it once was. It slows down considerably.

Love and Belonging

These are two separate genetic needs and as my Russian friend Sergei Bogolepov reminded me, one is unconditional while the other is conditional. Whether we tend to believe it or not, we humans have this need to love and to be loved. Love comes not only in the form of romantic love but also in the love that comes from friendships. As social animals, we also have the need to belong to many different possible groups i.e. church, professional organizations, clubs, schools, A.A., etc. including members of the human race.

Power

The word "power" usually conjures up visions of force. While force is used as a means of power with some people, power is also attained by being recognized and appreciated by others. Acceptance and appreciation are forms of power. Achievement and competing are also satisfying needs for power. If you can find a way that causes others to respect you, then you have found the greatest power you could possibly attain.

Freedom

Freedom is the ability to come and go as one pleases, to choose our own desires, and to make choices of our own volition; to live life free of encumbrances or imprisonment, either real or imagined.

Fun

Fun is how we learn. We don't necessarily do things that aren't fun. We like those things that are enjoyable. If you were to recall the subjects you enjoyed in school, it is almost a certainty that the teacher made the subject fun and/or was a subject you considered to be fun. We strive to have fun throughout all of our lives. The trips we take, the relationships we have, the games we play, the socializing we do, all have a genetic reward of learning. We learn about ourselves as well as other people, places, and things.

The aging process tends to chip away at these needs in our later years because they seem to be more permanent and lasting in nature due to incapacitation or limited physical abilities. Illness, poor health, and inadequate retirement income threatens our survival. A hazardous environment, in what used to be one's safe haven, may now exist due to poor mobility and loss of sight and hearing. No longer are we able to physically defend ourselves if need be. Both our survival and safety needs are compromised.

Over the years, we have created and saved many different tools to deal with our unhappiness. Some of these tools were handed down to us from our family by observing how they dealt with stress and unhappiness. We also have created our own personalized tools when none of the other tools were effective. Whatever the tool, be it an old standby or a newly created tool, the purpose of the tool is to ease or fix our unhappiness even if only a modicum of temporary relief. Primarily, we want it to resolve all of our unhappiness. When one newly created tool is ineffective, we use our creativity and imagination to create another tool to use to get the job done.

Pharmaceutical companies are making fortunes creating tools that ease unhappiness but don't cure the problem. Doctors and psychiatrists are often quick to hand these tools over to their patients. These tools only cover up one's unhappiness and behaviors by interfering with the brain's normal ability to be creative and resolve their unhappiness on their own.

When you see someone, whose behavior appears out of the ordinary, strange, or what you might call, "crazy." they are only using their creativity to satisfy one or more of their basic needs that are lacking the degree they wish to have of that/those needs so that the image of what they perceive outside of themselves closely matches the photo of the image they have inside their photo album.

Nothing can cause the loss of love more than death. A close second to death would be the conflict that may arise between loved ones and family members when someone dies. When one is in the Autumn of their years, other family members often become very interested in what shall become of a parent's or other family member's assets. Greed and contempt have been known to raise their ugly heads and distance family members resulting in anger, jealousy, grudges, loss of respect, and the loss of love. Unresolved conflict from the past that may have had an onset many years ago also depletes one's love and belonging needs. Common unresolved issues of the past are unacceptable behavior of one or more people in the family, feelings of betrayal, or taking advantage of others.

Retirement is a major loss of identity for a man as well as a sense of belonging, from the loss of a spouse. A woman's empty nest syndrome or loss of a loved one due to death may contribute to the loss of both love and belonging.

Society often perceives aging adults as losing their productive worth, becoming helpless, needy, or useless to society. These attitudes are reflected in ways in which society reacts to the elderly in such ways as rudeness, anger, controlling, and disgust. If someone were to behave like that towards you, you would not feel your power needs of respect, acceptance, and appreciation being met regardless of your age.

The loss of mobility, physical, and mental abilities, to accomplish the things that one used to do with ease can be extremely frustrating and lead to one's own loss of self-worth and happiness.

The need for freedom is also lost over time due to one's inability to drive safely. Loss of vision and the glare from oncoming lights of other drivers at night can be blinding and high risk for wrecking the car and/or even death. Reaction time slows down when faced with making a sudden move to avoid a collision or object. What used to be a simple task to do for ourselves may now require the assistance of others to help us.

Other family members may see the elderly parent as incapable of making his/her own decisions because they believe they know what's best for the parent more than the parent does. The loss of one's ability to make their own decisions or to go to places one wants to go, either because of physical hardship or the control of others, is another happiness destroyer of freedom needs for happiness.

If any or all of the above needs are not being met to the satisfaction of an aging person, there is little doubt that they are not having any fun in their life. There is little doubt that aging can, and often does, take its toll on those who are experiencing it. Aging can create unhappiness by the way one feels physically, how they perceive what is physically happening to them, how others may treat them, and how they may feel a loss of purpose or even failure.

Aging can just as easily provide a sense of happiness, satisfaction, and wellbeing. It all depends on the perception of the aging person.

Boredom And Alcohol/Drugs

A common situation with those who are retired, whose families have moved away, whose friends are no longer near or have deceased . . . is boredom. Boredom is a common happiness destroyer. With too much time on one's hands, there is a tendency for some to get into their heads and think unhappy thoughts . . . recalling all the times they have been hurt or wounded by others, both real and imagined. There are also the unwanted thoughts concerning their own mortality. Feeling sorry for one's self leads to thoughts of "Poor me. Poor me. Pour me another drink."

Nothing is as effective at ridding one's unwanted emotions as alcohol, street drugs, and/or the abuse and addiction to prescription drugs. In only a matter of a few seconds, alcohol and illicit drugs can numb the brain into a mental state of just not giving a damn about anything that may be bothering them. Some prescription drugs do the same thing but not as quickly as illicit drugs.

There are, however, a few people who consume alcohol or use amphetamine wherein just the opposite may occur. Their unhappiness and any anger may become exaggerated from the substance and intensify their emotions. They may even hallucinate and react in ways that may harm themselves or others. This is more commonly the case with amphetamine use.

I live in a state that caters to many retirees. We have many retirement communities throughout the state. Whenever Walgreens® advertises a sale on alcohol, the liquor shelves become empty extremely fast and the advertised products are often sold out by 9:00 AM.

Whenever individuals and neighbors of these communities, as well as their friends get together, the alcohol flows like water. Card games and other parlor games are often enjoyed or they may sit around and tell old war stories of their lives, or commiserate about their health or insurance. Whatever the activity, alcohol will be involved with the host pouring freely.

Just now, as I write this book, I got a call from a 66 year-old client who got a DUI in her home state of North Dakota. She is here in Arizona as one of our many annual snowbird visitors escaping the cold weather of their hometowns. She received a DUI in North Dakota after drinking several glasses of wine with a friend. On the way home, she hit a pickup truck (no injuries) but continued to drive home. Someone witnessed the incident and got her license plate number and reported the incident to the police who then went to her home and made the arrest. Her Blood Alcohol Content (BAC) was .24 which is three times the legal limit.

She reported during my assessment that both she and her husband no longer go out to drink at clubs or restaurants a couple of times a month. She said because they are retired, they now stay at home and drink three or four times a week with friends in the retirement community where they are currently staying for the winter.

She came to complete her court ordered alcohol and drug screen and Motor Vehicle Department evaluation here in Arizona for two reasons. The first reason is one of which she would admit: Get it over with to expedite the legal process to be able to be less stressed about it and put it behind her. The second reason is one which she would not be too willing to admit: Complete the process in Arizona so that she can avoid the embarrassment of those who know her back home of finding out about her arrest.

Many poor or serious health conditions are the result of heavy alcohol consumption which may be overlooked by doctors who are not familiar with recognizing the symptoms of abuse until it reaches the later stages of addiction. Another cause for misdiagnosing alcohol abuse is that the patient does not fully disclose how often and how much s/he consumes alcohol.

As a practitioner of an outpatient alcohol and drug treatment center, I only occasionally get clients for treatment that are over the age of 65. Most of my clients tend to be younger and fail to see their use as problematic. The much older clients whom I do see are those who have been referred to me for evaluation to see if they are safe to have their driver's license reinstated after two or more DUI charges. For the most part, those over 65 who have alcohol problems have been drinking for years and everyone looked the other way until it was too late. By then, the elder alcohol dependent person will require inpatient treatment rather than my outpatient clinic.

Because alcohol is legal and so widely used, many people are not aware of the symptoms of abuse or dependence (including the abuser/alcoholic). Most people would say that if a person drinks every day, they are an alcoholic. This is not necessarily true.

There are alcoholics who drink only once every few years. But when they do, they binge drink . . . consuming large amounts of alcohol at a time. A person who enjoys a drink or two after work every day is not necessarily an alcoholic. Nor is alcohol addiction a character disorder which so many people, including many doctors, believe it to be.

The 66 year-old female client I referenced earlier, while not currently biochemically addicted to alcohol, was shocked when I informed her that her current use was borderline . . . that she is currently abusing alcohol and if she were to continue drinking the way that she has been, that it won't be very long before she does cross that line into biochemical addiction. Will this information cause her to change her current pattern of use? Most likely, it won't. However, when she completes the outpatient treatment program that I referred her to, she *may* see the need at that time. Her retirement activities and living with an alcohol co-abusing husband will decrease the odds of her seeing a need to stop.

One of the difficulties for seniors to accept that they may be addicted to alcohol is that they perceive an alcoholic as a "skid row bum" laying in the gutter and homeless. Since that image doesn't match their own image, they refuse to accept the fact that they may have an alcohol problem. The truth is: Only 3% of alcoholics fit that "skid row" description. All others look just like you and me.

Drinking alcohol or using drugs is one of the most common tools I wrote about earlier that people use to deal with their unhappiness. The effectiveness of their use for this purpose is usually discovered very early in life.

Just what is an alcoholic? Someone is addicted to alcohol (or drugs) when they continue to drink or use the drug even though it causes problems. The next question would be, "what kind of problems?"

Here are the symptoms of alcohol abuse. The more of the abusive symptoms one has, the more they are likely to be addicted.

- Drinking four or more drinks in an hour.
- Drinking just after waking up.
- Their use has harmed relationships.

- Hiding their drinking from others to avoid getting into arguments with those who disapprove.
- Drinking/using alone. This is done to keep others from knowing how often and how much one drinks/uses.
- Hiding bottles in various parts of the house or garage or in a vehicle.
- Not recalling things said or done the night before after a drinking/using.
- Family and/or friends voice concerns about your drinking/using.
- Getting defensive or justifying your use when others talk to you about your drinking/using.
- Missing work due to use.
- Drinking/using on the job.
- Losing a job due to use.
- Drinking or using to deal with anger, disappointment, or depression.
- Waking the next morning with hands shaking even if just slightly.
- Drinking to ease the effects of a hangover.
- Regular use to get to sleep or to deal with pain.
- Mood swings when drinking/using.
- Arguments or fights when drinking/using
- Gulping the first few drinks.

- Getting two or more DUI charges.
- Passing out.
- Involvement of Domestic violence or disorderly conduct after drinking/using.

All alcoholics abuse alcohol. The only difference between an abuser and an addicted drinker is that the addicted drinker has a repeating drinking pattern with many of the above symptoms. The abuser experiences some of the symptoms but not in a regular pattern.

These behaviors are often seen by others but they fail to recognize them as problematic. The attitude is, "Doesn't everybody do this sometimes? The answer is "No." Normal drinkers do not display any of these abusive behaviors on a regular basis. Two or three "yes" responses to any of these behaviors are enough for one to take a close look at their drinking. More than three is definitely a serious concern.

The abuser also has an attitude that blinds them from seeing the seriousness of their use. They have been drinking to deal with their unhappiness for some time now and they have developed a relationship with it to the point that they don't want to even think about giving it up. They say to themselves and others, "I know my limits. And if my drinking starts to be a problem, I'll simply stop."

The problem with this thinking is that everyone else will see the drinker's use causing problems long before the alcoholic ever does. And if and when they do recognize their drinking is a problem, it is too late to just merely attempt to stop. Once the body has become bio-chemically conditioned, an intense outpatient or inpatient treatment will be required dependent upon the severity of any withdrawal symptoms.

Alcohol and drug addiction relapses often occur early upon cessation because the body's cellular structure has learned to function with a continual introduction of the substance in the body. The cells are now being deprived of it. This causes the cells to react violently causing a lot of physical discomfort and anxiety or depression. The drinker/user may rationalize a relapse because of the thought, "Hell! I felt better when I was drinking/using." So they relapse.

There are still two remaining factors to deal with in regard to alcohol/drug addiction. As difficult as it is to stop drinking, that is the easy part. The hard part is learning how to live without relying on drugs or alcohol to deal with one's stress and unhappiness. There may also be other aspects of social skills that may need to be developed that were never learned due to years of drinking or using. Abstinence is one thing. Recovery is yet another thing.

Incidentally, all unhappy people are unhappy about something that is going on right now . . . in the present. Alcoholics and addicts are unhappy about their present situation and not because of something that happened to them years ago. A person who is just now starting to drink heavily is doing so to deal with their current unhappiness.

If you suspect that you *might* have a drinking or drug problem, you probably do. Otherwise the thought wouldn't enter your mind. Make an appointment to be evaluated by a licensed alcohol/drug agency and not a medical doctor (unless s/he specializes in substance abuse). The evaluator will be able to see your specific needs and refer you, if necessary, to a program that will not recommend less or extend more treatment than you may need. There are outpatient and inpatient programs available dependent upon the severity of one's addiction.

As we age, our cells and organs begin to wear down and weaken through a process called oxidation. Yes, we get rusty in our old age. Regular consumption of alcohol will only increase the process. Alcohol has a shotgun effect on the body. It affects all organs and cells that you have. The two most common causes of death from alcohol are cirrhosis and pancreatitis. Alcohol also weakens the heart muscles so if you have a bad heart, alcohol is not your friend although several doctors may tell you otherwise.

You've Got to Manage Your Own Health Care

Patient: Doctor, it hurts when I raise my arm over my head.

Doctor: Then don't do that.

When it comes to physical health, most people put all their faith in their doctor. They put their lives totally in the hands of their doctor and do whatever s/he says without question. Like any profession, there are good plumbers and bad plumbers; good mechanics and poor mechanics. So it is with doctors. I don't wish to demean doctors in this book because many of them can and do save lives. But remember, the person who graduated last in his class in medical school is still called, "Doctor."

I have had several experiences with doctors over the years and it has been my misfortune to come across just as many of the poor doctors as the good. Doctors are not gods. They are human and make mistakes just like you and I do.

The medical field has become so specialized that no one doctor has the ability to treat each and every physical malady that people incur.   Doctors seek the pathology in order to make the diagnosis of your condition and then prescribe medications or refer you to a specialist who may have more knowledge or experience pertaining to the pathology and who may prescribe specific medication or perhaps even surgery.

A particular fact regarding medicine is: Very few medications have any curative abilities of any physical illness that isn't caused by an infection.   The medications prescribed for non-infectious conditions may ease the symptoms of the conditions but don't cure them.   In time the body may heal itself while the symptom-easing medications make it bearable to live with the problem.   On the downside are the things these medications do to your body and brain that you don't want them to do.   You know them as "side effects."

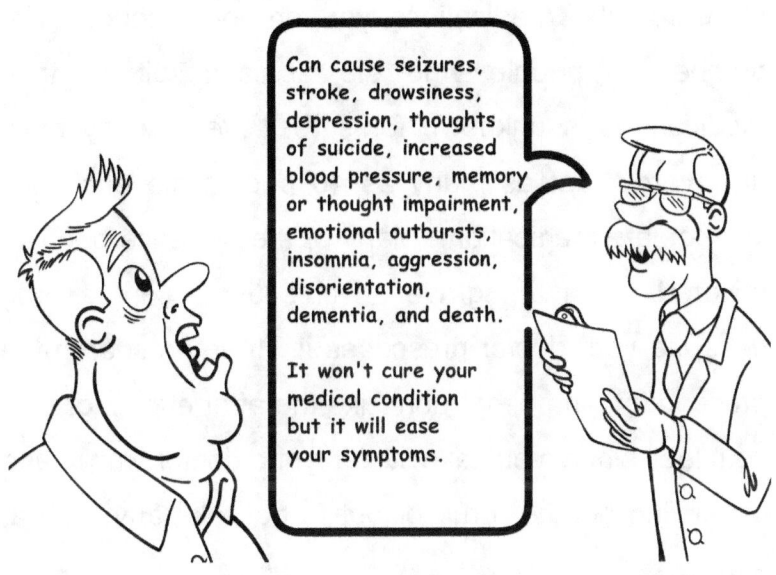

By regulation, the TV ads promoting drugs must inform the public of these side effects. I am amazed that people would even consider taking a drug whose side effects are often worse than the physical condition from which they suffer. Even when informed that the drugs could cause stroke or death, people will take these drugs mainly because "my doctor prescribed them" (the inference being that it's okay since a doctor said to take them). All drugs have side effects . . . even aspirin.

Ask questions regarding the instructions your doctor gives you. Take it upon yourself to learn as much as you can about your condition if it is serious enough.

Research the medications you are prescribed. The number of people who die as a result of their medications is unknown for sure. We recently have discovered that as many as 40 people die each day from opiate medication.[6] Many of the statistics become covered up in the grave. Don't just accept a drug because your doctor prescribes it. If you research the prescription and either don't like the after effects or how you feel when you take it, let your doctor know and either find another drug or opt to not take any drug at all.

Today's doctors' offices are busy around the clock. Doctors often see three or four patients at a time, hopping from one examination room to another. All this is going on while you are sitting in the waiting room long after your appointment time has passed. My good friend, Dr. Ken Larson, told me, "It takes 30 minutes for a doctor to explain a drug to a patient and only 30 seconds to write a prescription." Which direction do you think they most often choose?

---

[6]Retrieved from http://www.webmd.com/mental-health/addiction/news/20111101/40-us-deaths-a-day-from-prescription-painkillers

Be wary of the long-term use of medications made up of steroids, opiates, those that harm internal organs, those that have addictive capabilities, and many psych meds commonly being used for diagnoses of depression, bipolar, schizophrenia, and anxiety. What is being diagnosed as mental illness does not have any pathology. Doctors and psychiatrists may tell you that specific pathology exists for these behaviors only because this has been an ongoing myth since before the creation of psychiatry. While some doctors and psychiatrists may admit the lack of any pathology, they will still be quick to say, "We know it's there. We just haven't found it yet (for the last hundred years). *Parentheses mine.*

Prescription drug ads on TV seem to air second in frequency only to new car ads. Here are some drug ads that have been running on TV. **All** of these drugs have effects that you don't want. Those in bold *italics* have been taken off the air due to severe side effects:[7]

---

[7]Aubuchon, Vaughn P. Medicine Summaries Prescription Drugs - Prescription Drug TV Ads. Retrieved from http://www.vaughns-1-pagers.com/medicine/prescription-drug-tv-ads.htm#fosamax

Acetonel®	Detrol®	*Paxil*®	Viagra®
Actos®	Levitra®	*Plavix*®	*Vioxx*®
Avodart®	Lunesta®	Premarin®	*Vytorin*®
Boniva®	Nexium®	Prilosec®	*Wellbutrin*®
Celebrex®	Ditropan®	*Procrit*®	*Zelnorm*®
Cialis®	Enbrel®	Strattera®	Zocor®
Coreg®	*Fosamax*®	Valtrex®	*Zyprexa*®
Crestor®	Humira®	Vesicare®	Jublia®
Xarelto®	Victoza®		

One might be inclined to ask, "Why would these drugs that have been removed from TV been advertized in the first place?" One of the reasons is that the FDA accepts the in-house research findings from the makers of these drugs as being complete and accurate when they are wrong or misleading. And while the pharmaceutical companies claim that much of their profits go towards research and development, they actually go towards advertising.

TV networks are not drug researchers and they, too, assume the maker's drugs are safe because it is supposedly the responsibility of the pharmaceutical companies and the FDA to insure their safety. The networks also are very aware that drug companies spend megabucks in advertising so they give preference to the drug companies. Pharmaceutical companies are continually being sued and are paying vast sums of money, out-of-court, on the condition that if the patient discloses how much they are being paid, they will no longer receive any money. Hush money.

You may wish to take a serious look at your medications if your medicine cabinet contents are worth more than your bank account.

There are yet other reasons why you must manage your own health and not blindly accept what you may be prescribed. Out of all of the drugs being advertised on television perhaps the only one with curative abilities is Jublia® for toenail fungus. If you don't have prescription insurance, Jublia could cost as much as $700.00. If you do have insurance, it may be $250.00. All other drugs only cover up the symptoms to varying degrees and can cause other harm to your health.

For those who swear their psych meds helped them, several major studies have proven that a placebo or sugar pill has been just as effective, if not more, than drugs that have been created to treat conditions that have no physical pathology. At best, these drugs simply drug the user's brain, affecting all of their emotions that lead to their unhappiness and subsequent maladaptive behavior. Remember the Total Behavior concept mentioned earlier? There is not one drug that can go to any one area to isolate one single and specific unwanted emotion. If one emotion is drugged, all emotions are drugged.

Most of all, these drugs inhibit one's ability to be creative. Creativity is what we rely on to overcome our unhappiness without the use of drugs. It is our creativity that we use to try any number of ways to deal with our unhappiness and frustration without the use or need for medication.

The average person is able to overcome their depression in six weeks or less. Why do many practitioners inform their patients that the antidepressant they have been prescribed may take up to six weeks before it begins to take effect? And why would patients be told that they must take psych meds for the rest of their life for a medical condition that doesn't exist?

Spellbinding

Another factor of medication is a condition that Dr. Peter Breggin refers to as "Spellbinding." Spellbinding is the term he uses to describe how a psychiatric medication may cause some modicum of relief for anxiety, depression, schizophrenia, et al. This numbing or mind-altering the brain can be seen as false "improvements." He states that the drug-induced apathy or euphoria created by the drug is misinterpreted as an improvement. He further states that the brain has been partially disabled and changes the individual's mood causing patients less able to feel, perceive, or express their underlying mental condition or outlook, and their inability to see their adverse effects or their emotional problems.[8]

I find this same phenomenological form of behavior in alcohol and drug dependent individuals as a contributing factor in an addict's denial that they have a drug or alcohol problem or that their use is affecting others. They are using alcohol and drugs to self-medicate. The drugs/alcohol numb the brain too. Patients, addicts, alcoholics, when drinking or taking

---

[8]Peter Breggin, "Medication Madness," 2008, pp 27, 28, ST. Martin Press, New York, NY

drugs for unhappiness, become apathetic and "just don't give a damn" as long as their drug or alcohol is in their bodies and brains. Added to the spellbinding effect is something called anosognosia: A condition of behaving in ways that others can see as problematic but the person taking the medication fails to see.

Criteria have been developed for recognizing or determining if any extreme or unusual behavior is drug-induced. The criteria apply to not only prescription psychiatric medications but to street drugs as well.

- A recent change (up or down) in the dose of the medication;
- A relatively sudden onset of rapid escalation;
- Escalating symptoms of drug toxicity, such as Insomnia, agitation, memory dysfunction, hallucinations, or other abnormal behaviors leading up to the event;
- An unusually violent, irrational, bizarre, or self-defeating quality to the behavior;
- An obsessive, compelling, and unrelenting quality to the behavior;
- A prior history indicating that the abnormal behaviors were uncharacteristic and unprecedented before exposure to the drug;

- The individuals subjective feeling that the feelings and actions are alien, inexplicable, and ethically repugnant;
- Gradual disappearance of the abnormal mental state after stopping the medication (although some residual effects may last much longer).[9]

Once a person has been taking a drug for any long period of time, their body (or brain) has become accustomed to the presence of this drug and has learned to accept it. Should a patient decide to stop taking their medication, the body will react in the form of withdrawal. The cells are no longer receiving the elements of the drug in their body and the cells react in such a way as to cause many types of symptoms. These symptoms range from anxiety, sweating, nausea, inability to sleep, irritability, diarrhea, epilepsy, strokes, and even death. All it takes is for any one of these withdrawal symptoms to lead the patient into thinking, "Hell, I felt much better when I was taking the drug." So they immediately return to taking the drug. This is also why so many drug addicts and alcoholics relapse.

---

[9]Ibid, p 373

Yet another component of spellbinding is the resolution of whatever was contributing to one's unhappiness having resolved on its own over time while the patient believes it was the medication that made it better. And again, if they ever attempt to stop taking their medication, they experience the withdrawal of the medication which they feel only confirms the false efficacy of the medicine.

Prescription drug addiction has been increasing each and every year. The most common of these drugs are the opiates such as Percocet®, Percodan®, Hydrocodone®, Oxycodone®, Oxycontin®, Lyrica®, Codeine®, and Darvon®. These drugs are commonly prescribed for pain that many doctors seem to prescribe like Pez dispensers.

Besides blocking pain receptors in the brain, these drugs tend to increase endorphins and dopamine which gives the sensation of pleasure that encourages repetition of use. Continued use increases tolerance to the drug and more of the drug is needed to get the desired effect. I have had clients who started out on 5 mg of Vicodin® per day who ended up taking as much as 5 pills of 10 mgs, 5 or more times per day. Vicodin®

94

also contains 300mg of Acetaminophen per pill which has been known to lead to liver failure and even death. If taking ten or more Vicodin® tablets a day, you are taking at least 3,000 mg or more, of acetaminophen per day.

The use of alcohol with any opiate drug quickens the harm done to the liver. When I do alcohol and drug intakes, one of the questions I ask is if the client has ever thought about or attempted suicide. Many will tell me "no" but later admit to drinking alcohol while taking drugs that in combination could easily kill them. When they disclose that they drink while on these drugs, I state, "I thought you told me you didn't have any suicidal ideations or attempts."

Drinking alcohol on opioid drugs is a common cause of death. Even when I give them this information, it has little effect towards getting them to stop. Why? Their thoughts are, "Well it hasn't killed me yet." Even when advised by their doctor not to drink on their medication, they pay this warning little heed. That's the power of addiction. It is also proof that information will not necessarily cause anyone to behave differently.

No opiate drug should be taken when the patient is also taking Xanax or other antidepressant drugs. Doing so has the effect of synergism that increases the pleasure effects of the drug for a longer and greater "high." This is common practice of Heroin users along with other opiate drugs. It's dangerous and is quite often fatal.

WARNING: DO NOT STOP TAKING ANY MEDICATION THAT YOU HAVE BEEN PRESCRIBED TO TAKE WITHOUT THE SUPERVISION OF YOUR DOCTOR.

You've also got to manage your own medical bills as well. Don't merely accept what a billing company may bill you without checking the validity of the bill. I have caught several incorrect fees by cross-referencing my payments to what the bill says I paid (or didn't pay). This advice applies not only to a service provider but any Medicare advantage or supplemental plan you may have.

LIVE THE LIFE YOU WANT

It would be very easy for me to continue writing and offer you all sorts of platitudes about aging. They wouldn't be anything that you haven't already heard others say hundreds of times or seen on social Internet sites. To ease the pain of aging and any unhappiness, you can only do things that come from within your own mind and your own internal beliefs. No one can do them for you but I can show you what so many people before you report were or are the criteria for living happy the last years of their life.

1. **ACCEPTANCE**

   Growing older is not anything you can fight or control. You may be able to slow it down or temporarily cover it up but you will not be able to stop it. Stop trying to fight it.

2. **GRATITUDE**

   Be thankful for all that you have experienced in your life . . . the unhappy times as well as the happy times. They brought you knowledge and awareness about others as well as yourself. Be thankful for all that you have. Whatever your situation in life, it could always be worse.

   Be grateful for waking each morning for the opportunity to enjoy life and living another day.

One day you could wake up and find that you died in your sleep.

George Burns said, "When I get up in the morning, the first thing I do is read the obituaries. If my name isn't there, I have breakfast."

Be thankful for whatever you may have lost financially, materialistically, and in relationships. Most aging people come to realize that all of the things they used to struggle to acquire in their life no longer hold any importance or meaning to them except for their past and present relationships. As Dr. Seuss has said, "Don't cry because it's over, smile because it happened."

Even the worst relationships you may have had with others had a payoff of something good that came from them. Only you would know what those things are if you would take the time to think about them. Your relationship with them wasn't all bad all of the time. There were some good times even in the worst of marriages and relationships that came to be for all the wrong reasons.

Expressing gratitude for all of the things in your life will require at least one other person with whom you have a meaningful relationship. For those who may have lost all of their close friends for any reason, they will still need to express being grateful to someone or some entity to gain any result or satisfaction from being grateful.

3. **FAITH**

This is not a chapter to convert anyone to any religion. If you are currently a religious person or someone who decided to put it all behind you but now feel you would like it to be back in your life, then this section is for you. If you are agnostic or atheistic, then move on to # 4.

Faith is something that can give you strength and courage to move on with your life when all else and/or everyone else has not been there for you. Your belief in a better life can be comforting in your final days. Can I prove there is an afterlife? No. I can't. Nor can I prove that an afterlife doesn't exist. As for me . . . I would rather believe and be wrong than not believe and find out differently.   Faith gives hope for the impossible and strength to overcome hardships.

Mostly, having Faith in a Higher Power allows you to profess your gratitude to the one entity that matters.   Whatever you may have in your life: Your home, your family, your friends, your belongings, your career, your finances, etc . . . you have been blessed.   There are so many more people in the world who don't have anywhere near what you have been blessed to have.

4. **BELIEFS**

Those things that we believe both true and false, shape the person we become and further determine our life's choices.   As Shakespeare wrote, "There is no right or wrong. Only thinking makes it so."   Those who believe they can maintain a healthy lifestyle that involves meaningful relationships and satisfies our Basic Needs as well as giving back to others tend to have longer and more satisfying lives than those who think and feel otherwise. If you feel that you are on a downhill ride, there is a definite tendency to make choices and create a lifestyle that will support that belief. You will actually be making choices and living a lifestyle that will bring about the end of your life sooner than need be. The thoughts you have determine the choices you make.

5. **STAY ACTIVE**

   Exercise Regularly – Stop-eating foods that contribute to heart disease, cancer, and diabetes.

   Processed meats, white flour, sugar, corn oil, and tobacco are foods that scrape and scar the interior of your arteries that allows cholesterol to adhere to them. As I stated earlier, most people die due to the things they've been putting in their mouths. Instead, opt for lean meats and fish, olive oil, colorful fruits and vegetables.

   Begin a routine of walking at least three times a week or more with two to three thousand steps or more per exercise. Utilize the equipment at your local gym that your Medicare advantage program may cover.

Review the prescription drugs you have been taking. Some blood pressure meds as well as drugs utilizing steroids often cause harmful side effects that are not good for your health. Long-term use of opiate pain medications most likely have become an addiction and harmful to your liver and other organs. Psychiatric medications such as antidepressants and those used for those who suffer from anxiety are not healthy for you in any way. They cure nothing yet are successful in numbing your emotions and keeping your brain from functioning normally as well as affecting your ability to interact with others in loving, caring, and empathetic ways while not being able to recognize these effects.

Several of the clients I have seen who came to me while having been on several different drugs, have stopped taking them only to find they had more energy and felt much happier in life. They weaned themselves off of their drugs with the help of their primary care physician. Taking certain drugs necessitated by your physical illnesses should not to be stopped suddenly. Question your doctor's explanation for why you may be taking so many drugs especially when taking more than one drug for the same ailment. Taking psychotic medications for conditions in which you have no psychosis and are being used for other symptoms are to be seriously questioned. Blood pressure and cholesterol problems can be better treated with diet and exercise than medications that have harmful side effects. I have seen clients who are taking so many different drugs that their doctor even gave them another drug to deal with the side effects of all the others that they are taking.

Another client of mine reported that his doctor had him sign a disclaimer for any liability should the patient become addicted to the drug the doctor was prescribing.

Some withdrawal symptoms from medications can lead to seizures, strokes, and even death.

AGAIN: DO NOT STOP TAKING ANY MEDICATION YOU HAVE BEEN PRESCRIBED FOR ANY CONSIDERABLE AMOUNT OF TIME WITHOUT THE SUPERVISION OF A MEDICAL DOCTOR.

6. HAVE A REASON TO SURVIVE

Have reason(s) to be safe, to love and be loved, to belong, to be free, to have fun, to be respected, to accomplish, and to be appreciated.

Wow!! What else is there? These are the things that give meaning to your life. Just because you may be retired doesn't mean you retire from living. When you retire, you can be bitter or you can be better. Life and living doesn't stop just because you no longer have a career, a family, or the physical agility you used to have. Without a purpose, you may as well sit in your recliner and watch mindless TV all day. Be active. Volunteer. Socialize. Garden. Create. Build. What you see is what you will get. If you see yourself as old and decrepit, your life will reflect the same.

You can sit around and feel sorry for yourself or bemoan the mistakes you made in your life and deal with them with drugs or alcohol. You can hold grudges and be angry at yourself or others. Or you can suck up your aches and pains, get out of the grandstands and get in the arena and participate in the game of life.

None of the suggestions I offer above are beneficial if you don't have at least one meaningful relationship in your life. And the more meaningful relationships you have, the happier you will be while applying and possessing the guidelines above.

Dealing With The Death Of Loved Ones

The death of those who are closest to us can be very emotionally devastating. Grief is unavoidable if you are at all human. When it happens unexpectedly, it's a great shock and hard to accept. If due to a long illness and is expected, it is still difficult to accept, but perhaps not as shocking.

Grief

Grief is depression and a normal emotion to experience with the loss of someone or something near and dear to us. The deeper the love for a person, it seems the deeper the grief when they die.

Grief is the price we pay for love.

The death of those we love often causes us to be more aware of our own mortality and impending demise.

Grief (depression) is not a chemical imbalance of the brain as the world has been fooled into believing. It is a natural response to a deeply unhappy situation. In the case of death, it is the loss of life of someone whom we don't want to lose. It could be said that much of our grief is a matter of self-centeredness . . . deep sadness for our own loss of that person. We no longer have someone in our life that we want to be there.

Breakups and divorce commonly lead to depression as well. Again, it is because of our own personal loss. But the loss of someone due to death is such a permanent and final act with no return or hope for reconciliation. It is the bold exclamation point signifying the end of a person's life and that they are now physically gone from our life forever. This bit of awareness and reality, in itself, is a hard pill to swallow.

Doctors and psychiatrists tend to treat depression as a mental illness even though it has no physical pathology. The common treatment is a prescription for an antidepressant which is a drug that has no curative abilities but will numb the brain from feeling emotions and empathy as well as keeping the brain from functioning the way it is supposed to function normally.

Depression and sadness are the result of whatever we ruminate with unhappy thoughts. It can affect us not only emotionally but physically as well. Depression can lead to lowering your body's immunity. It can add stress to internal organs that may already have a preconditioned weakness or malady. It can be totally debilitating to say the least.

Dr. Glasser, the creator of Realty Therapy and Choice Theory, explains how depression is a choice. When I share this information with others, they look at me as if I have lost my mind. They believe it is a physical condition of which they have no control. Actually, the truth is, they are controlling the onset of their own depression when they suffer from it. Allow me to explain Dr. Glasser's findings about depression having helped thousands of clients in his lifetime and without once ever prescribing medication.

Depression is an emotion that is chosen for the purpose of finding some form of deep emotional relief even if the relief is minimal. Since it is a choice, it is an activity which indicates it is a verb or gerund, and not an adjective or a noun. He refers to it as one who is "choosing to depress" or "one who is depressing." He further explains that choosing to depress serves any one or more of three ways to ease their unhappiness.

1. Choosing to depress often serves the purpose of getting others to come to us when we are the neediest and wish consolation so as not to have to suffer alone. It is a way of asking for help without verbally asking for help.

   I'm sure you can relate to times of your own deep sadness when your body and facial expressions indicated your unhappiness even when you may have tried to hide it. Others came to you and asked, "Are you okay?" "Is everything alright?" "Is something wrong?" Most likely, you have even approached others with the same questions when you noticed someone else who was appearing sad and dejected. You came to their aid just as others came to yours.

2. Choosing to depress can also serve the purpose of keeping you from choosing to feel anger. The interesting thing about depressing and angering is that you cannot do both at the same time. You can do one or

the other but you can't do both simultaneously.

Another interesting aspect about depressing and angering is that when it comes to dealing with the death of a loved one, we may often ping-pong from choosing to depress and choosing to anger. We get angry at any number of things when we try to make sense of death. We can get angry with God (what an ego *that* takes), angry towards the person we lost for leaving us; angry because of our loss of that person; angry at life and thoughts of "It's not fair!" We can also choose to become angry with those who try to cheer us up. Even with the best intent of our friends, it is not uncommon to lash out at them verbally because "You have no idea how or what I am feeling right now! Leave me alone!" The message is, "I need you right now, get away from me!"

When we see that our anger may be harming others, or even ourselves, we choose to return to depressing so that we won't be angry.   Depressing keeps our angering in check.   Anger   is   expressing   one's unhappiness   outwardly.   Depression   is expressing one's unhappiness inwardly.

Moving in and out of anger and sadness is a part of the grieving process.   Let it happen and don't attempt to fight it.   Just don't let your anger be too intense, last too long, occur too frequently, or bring possible harm to yourself or others.

3. This next reason why people choose to depress is the major culprit in choosing to depress. The third reason has two parts to it:

The unhappy situation is one that we are not willing to accept as a reality because it does not, and cannot match the image in our mental photo album of how we want things to be.   It is a refusal to accept the reality of the situation (loss) knowing that there's not a thing we can do about it to change it.
You know there is something that you need to do to overcome your sadness but

111

a. You don't want to do it or

b. You don't know how to do it.

When someone close to us dies, we may not be ready to give up feeling our loss because it would mean having to dim the image we have of them in our photo album and we don't want to do that. Even though they may be deceased they will never totally be out of our photo album. Our memories of them will stay with us forever. Our memories of those whom we loved and lost are what keep their soul in our hearts and mind.

Knowing that we have to "let go" is not an easy thing to do but we know we will have to do so if we ever want to feel happy again. Letting go is not the letting go of the person, but letting go of the unhappiness.

The way we let go is to accept the reality of the situation. Acceptance allows us to move on without all of the pain that we had been feeling for our loss. Acceptance is something that comes at different times for different people. It doesn't mean that you love the departed person less because you are beginning to feel better. Your love for them will always be the same.

What will be less will be the pain and suffering you experienced to express your loss and unhappiness.

Looking back on those whom you have lost over the years will remind you of how you were able to eventually rise above the sadness you felt back then. It took some time but you got there. You will experience some happy days and sad days along the path to acceptance. It's easier to rise above depressing when you know it is a choice.

Everyone deals with grief in their own way and in their own time. How long or how short the grieving process depends on the individual. Over the years, I have learned to deal with it based upon the knowledge I have acquired from Dr. Glasser's Reality Therapy and Choice Theory.

As you may recall, I dedicate this book to my very good friend Dr. Ken Larsen who recently passed away. Knowing that I have a choice on choosing my emotions and how I want to feel, I have been able to avoid periods of deep mourning over his death. Those who are in recovery or are addiction clinicians might be inclined to say that I am in denial and refusing to allow my emotions to express themselves and to "work through the pain." As the saying goes in recovery circles, "The only way out of the pain is through the pain." That's what I used to believe in the past because that is what I had been taught. I now know, because of Choice Theory, that this is not true at all.

We all have the ability to choose how we want to feel. Yes, sorrow is a human emotion and without it, one would not be easily considered to be human or humane. How long and how intense we mourn or experience sorrow is a choice. I think of my friend every day since his passing. My thoughts are of gratitude for having known him and what I had gained by knowing him. When his memory comes to me, I automatically control my choice of emotions to be good emotions and not those that would make me sad and bring me down.

Occasionally, and very rarely, I purposely allow my sadness to come into play while knowing that I don't intend to stay there very long or to feel too intently over the loss of our daily communication. Allowing myself to feel the loss of my friend reminds me that I am human and miss his company that we had online each day. It keeps his memory alive which, in some philosophies, keeps his soul alive. I choose how deeply I wish to mourn while not allowing my emotions to bring me down or enter into a depressive state. This is the beauty of Choice Theory. I don't wish to feel miserable and depressed. Nor would my friend want me to feel miserable and depressed.

You may be thinking, "How do you do that? How can you control your emotions? Don't they just happen beyond anyone's control?" The answer is, "No." Your emotions are the result of whatever it is that you are thinking or doing. We don't have direct control of our emotions or, for that matter, our physiology. If I asked you to be truly elated right now . . .so ecstatically happy that you just beamed with enthusiasm, could you do it? You might act the part but you wouldn't be feeling the real emotion . . . only acting. If I were to ask you to break out in a cold sweat right now or have an allergy attack, could you do so on request? We don't have direct control of our emotions or our physiology but we do have direct control of our thoughts and our behavior.

Between stimulus and response there is a space. In that space is our power to choose our response. In our response lies our growth and our freedom.

Viktor E. Frankl

Since it is our thoughts and behavior that affects our emotions and physiology, the only way we can control our emotions and physiology is by way of the things in which we do have control. We can always change our thoughts and our behavior but we have no direct control of our emotions and physiology without our thoughts and behavior. You always have the power to change what you think and do . . . always. What you think and how you behave directly affects your emotions and physiology.

The key to overcoming any sorrow, soon after the initial shock or letdown, is to eventually come to the **reality** of the situation and **accept** the fact that there is nothing you can do to change it and that it is what it is. Once you have come to this point, you can continue to either feel miserable or grateful. This will only happen when you are willing to make this choice and no one can tell you when to do it or how long it will take you to get there. It's a choice you will make eventually, whether you do it now or months or years later. How long you are willing to suffer in sadness is up to you.

When a pilot of a small plane finds himself in a storm, he has two choices: He can fly all around the storm looking for a way out and burn up all of his fuel and crash, or he can continue in a straight course and eventually come out of the storm with enough fuel to carry on.

Detachment

It has been my experience that both men and women can sometimes isolate and detach from everyone when they lose a spouse. They forego their friends except, perhaps, for a family member or two. Some do it to deal with their deep depression while others do so in a form of resignation from life and others. They refuse offers from others who urge them to get out and be social. They usually have a list of alibis they give to justify their refusal to get together.

I have also experienced widows who were not all that happy with the marriage in the first place yet hung on for years due to financial, religious, or social-generational reasons. The loss of their spouse does not appear to be as great a loss of those whose marriage remained loving and meaningful.

Others may show their grief and seek empathy from strangers by informing them of their recent loss and do so in inappropriate places such as the checkout line at the grocery store for sympathy, or a social gathering in which they didn't want to be in the first place. The latter being a possible excuse to leave or to gain sympathy.

Single Seniors

There are hundreds of thousands of single seniors who found themselves alone after the death of their lifelong mate. After mourning, some may seek a new relationship or marriage while others may avoid it at all costs. Then there are those who attempt to avoid the pain of the loss of a spouse by seeking an immediate connection, or several connections, with another person or people to fill the void. The Internet is a source of several different "dating" programs that are intended to bring senior singles together. There are also many individuals, more women than men it would appear, who prefer to stay single for different reasons. I don't wish to infer that they are lonely.

Being alone and being lonely are two different things.

It would also appear that the needier a person is for a relationship, the more likely they may be to get involved for all the wrong reasons and with all the wrong people. The following are some observations that I have made from my own experiences as well as those clients and associates who have shared their experiences with me to include in this chapter.

I have been single, by divorce, since 1983. Since then, I have had several relationships that lasted anywhere from three to five years but none any longer than that. Why did they end? Some ended because we were not suitable matches in the first place. Others ended due to my own personal growth and awareness and for self-improvement and happiness. In other words, I was changing . . . growing so to speak . . . while my partners were uncomfortable with the changes I was making in my life. I was turning into a different person than they had originally met. A couple of women had substance abuse problems and when I overcame my own abuse, my abstinence threatened their continued use. They would end these relationships out of their own shame and guilt and/or fear of having to stop their drinking as well.

Some had expectations that they never communicated and when it looked like those expectations would never become real, they would end the relationship. They failed to communicate what they wanted or hoped for in the relationship and when it looked like it wasn't going to happen, they ended it with no explanation as to why.

I know of one instance where a woman felt intimidated about her partner's education and her lack of the same. Having hidden the secret of her unfinished education for years led to great anxiety and fear of being "discovered" and even outright bursts of anger (fear), when socializing with any new friends in simple conversation. It takes a lot of stress and energy to hide one's perceived shortcomings or shameful past from others. Thus comes the saying, "We're as sick as our secrets." When a person finally gives up all unsuccessful efforts trying to control or change another person, even the little things they may have tolerated or overlooked will now be considered major issues that can give cause and motivation to end the relationship.

Some would attempt to change me to suit their wants and needs without regard to accepting who I currently was or what we needed in a healthy relationship. Their methods to attempt to change me would result in what I refer to as the Seven Distancing Behaviors . . . a somewhat different name Dr. Glasser identified to describe controlling methods which he calls the Seven

Deadly Habits. The most commonly used methods to change someone are:

Criticizing	Blaming	Complaining
Nagging	Threatening	Punishing
	Bribing or Rewarding	

Any one of these behaviors will distance a person from another person rather than bring them closer together. In relationships with others, rarely is only one of these controlling behaviors used without the inclusion of another. When a person applies any of these behaviors on another person, the person on the receiving end tends to utilize them back to the person who originally began the process. Each time a distancing behavior is used, it causes respect and love to be chipped away until all love and respect is eventually gone.

If you feel you have to change someone and refuse to accept him or her for who and how they are in the present, then you will either have to end the relationship or change what you want and change how you behave towards them if you want the relationship to continue. Continued use of any of the Seven Distancing Behaviors will lead to loss of respect for each other, which, in turn, causes the loss of love.

If someone in your life is behaving in a manner in which you disapprove, the first person who needs to change is yourself. When you cease doing whatever you have been doing to attempt to change another person, they will stop doing whatever they have been doing to resist your control.

Looking back on my past relationships, I am grateful for all of them as well as having the hindsight to recognize that we are both better off having ended them. Those who know that I am single, currently not in a relationship, and living alone, often assume that I am lonely. To them, my non-involvement in a relationship or marriage is perceived as loneliness. Since they would imagine how they would feel living alone, they assume that others would feel the same. It reminds me of the story of the mother in a supermarket with her young child. While walking down the frozen food aisle, she might say to her child, "I'm cold. Put your sweater on." My living alone is a choice at this point in my life which could change at any time.

As I have often said, loneliness and being lonely are not the same thing. It's not like I live in a cave or that I have cut myself off from all of society. I have several associates as well as friends all over the world. They are friends who offer emotional support when needed and we share our joys and sorrows with each other. We would be there for each other at the drop of a hat if need be.

Would I like to have a relationship or marriage? Sure. But I have been single for a long time and have developed a single lifestyle and freedom that I would find a bit difficult to give up. For the right person, I would be willing to forfeit some of those freedoms. This holds true for anyone who is in a relationship. Whenever we become involved with another person, there are certain freedoms that will need to be forfeited in order to sustain the relationship.

Most of my contacts with other people are with my clients. In my business, I would not consider a mental health agency to be a wise location to find someone for a relationship. The last thing I want in a relationship is to be a therapist in that relationship. It would also be very unethical in my profession and I am not willing to jeopardize my license or my career for a relationship with a client. It seems that the women I am attracted to are either already married and have acquired relationship wisdom over the years or they are too young and we differ in education, interests, and values. Couples are drawn to one another by their shared interests. Relationships are sustained by their shared values.

Dating and Social Media Dating Sites

I have signed up for three or four dating sites over the years with each of them being pretty much the same thing: Needy and lonely women looking for a man to support them and/or direct their lives and make decisions for them. There are some who are controllers and demand their mate be a certain way or "forget it". There were others who are comfortable with who they are but their values conflicted with my values. One or both would begin to get the other person to change their values to match their own. The result would be a loss of respect by trying to control one another. It is best to avoid getting involved with someone of this ilk while thinking that you can change them down the road while believing that they can serve your wants and needs in the interim.

I no longer subscribe to these dating sites. I have met some very nice people on one or two of these sites, but they were all long distance and not conducive to maintaining a lasting relationship. I have also met some real doozies as well.

One had a PhD and after meeting for lunch decided she wanted to come meet with me right in my home. She got lost following the instructions on her GPS and kept looking for my home in a community where I didn't even live. Even when I gave explicit directions from where she currently was, she still failed to come to the right address right next to the community to where she was. A doctorate degree is not proof of intelligence. She is one of two women whom I had just met who wanted to meet with me alone in my home. A woman who is willing to go to a man's home without really knowing him is taking a major risk for her own safety.

The other woman who wanted to come to my home after meeting me for lunch, did so and while there, she disclosed she was currently married. She reported that she was not happy in the marriage and that it was okay with her husband that she could see other men. It wasn't okay with me.

Other women would appear suitable for a possible relationship after having traded several E-mails or even phone conversations. We all want to put our best foot forward when meeting someone. But after only one get-together over lunch or dinner, either I or she would see that we were not suited due to any number of differences or attitudes and neither of us willing to "settle" out of neediness. Consequently, we would both move on with no intent to want to change the other person and wished each other well. After meeting with some of these online dating sites, there have been just as many women who were not interested in me as I have been not interested in them. Being a counselor doesn't help matters either. Counselors and therapists tend to easily see any red flags that may be going on in someone's life. Consequently, some are intimidated by my profession.

Many of the photos that a person posts of themselves on these sites indicate they have little regard for their appearance which often indicates poor self-esteem. Still others rely on trying to lure a man with photos of them in lingerie, sitting on a bed, or proudly displaying their cleavage (or other perceived assets) while fully dressed. While these photos may attract a man, for all the wrong reasons, any resultant relationship would not be a very meaningful one. Both men and women have posted photos of themselves when they were younger and looked more attractive than they currently do.

Jan Milligan Angel, a high school classmate of mine, who now lives on the East Coast, gave me her insight and that of several of her widowed and single lady friends, in regard to their experiences with senior men seeking women online.   Jan, a widow, writes: "The common opinion that my friends and I share is that senior men are a bit delusional about their own age and appearance. While we all expect to change as we grow older, women are more accepting of physical changes and the importance of appearance in a companion is not a priority."

She further says, "Men approach women as romantic partners and are often times explicit about sexual expectations while women are interested in companionship and limited interest in marriage and romance. Older women, especially those who have been happily married and lost their longtime spouses, are offended by someone looking for "The love of their life" in their 70s. This seems to be a common thread on the web sites that we saw. There seemed to be a long list of expectations from the men seen on the dating sites which we found to be entertaining and laughable. Women want someone to share a movie, conversation, and dinner."

"Young women want marriage and usually a family. They want to build a family and life with someone. Older woman have already completed this desire and are not interested in repeating it. They are often financially secure and have a family. All that is missing is companionship. Perhaps men wish to recreate the comfortable life they had before their wives died. Or they may want to find romance that is more idealistic than it is realistic to have."

"Another factor to consider," she says, "is that those of us who lost a husband we loved after a long term illness are not eager to be hurt again and commit to that kind of loss. At our age, one or the other, or both of us, will have health issues so there is a fear of repeating the painful experiences and loss all over again. I actually saw an ad from a man on the dating site that said he wasn't interested in anyone with any health issues. He was 76!"

Meaningful relationships are a necessary component of possessing and maintaining happiness. However, those meaningful relationships don't necessarily have to be romantic or sexual in nature. They don't even have to be of opposite genders. Platonic relationships in lieu of romantic relationships can be very satisfying. Both romantic and platonic relationships are better than one or the other, alone. As long as you have at least one meaningful relationship, platonic or romantic, you will have some happiness in your life. And the more meaningful relationships you have, the more happiness you will have.

There are both men and women who, for various reasons, do not wish to have a meaningful relationship.

They make up for it by having pets while others may compensate through their connection and love of God or Christ via their faith. These relationships are always unconditional and meet their genetic need for love and belonging when they choose to avoid relationships with others. However, they fall short in fulfilling the need we have for social interaction with others. Still . . . they are better than no relationships at all.

There are both men and women who are left without adequate finances when a spouse dies or even after divorce. It is not uncommon for either gender to seek a relationship that is primarily based upon filling this unmet survival need of financial security. Again, if this is one's sole or primary goal for seeking a relationship, regardless of age, the relationship has little hope for lasting.

Men may want someone to care for them physically and financially in their later years after their wife died or after a divorce. These men are seeking a nurse with a purse.

An 89-year-old man met an 80-year-old woman at a retirement center. After a brief period of dating, they decided to get married. He spent his honeymoon getting out of the car.

Knowing When To Say "When"

There eventually comes a time when, even with the best of intentions, that continuing to work after retirement age is no longer effective. Physical, emotional, and perhaps some mental conditions no longer allow for performing up to your previous abilities. I have always been one who never had any inclination to ever retire or stop my career. I have the image in my photo album of myself counseling, writing, speaking, and helping people to empower their lives until I could no longer do so. While this may appear to be a noble image and cause, it can also be a form of denial or refusal to accept that the time may have come when it would be best to edit that photo album image.

Perhaps, like you, I have encountered the diminishing effects of aging. I ignore the typical aches and pains of aging and accept them as a normal part of life. I was not about to allow them to get in my way of continuing to be active and effective in my work. The reality is, if it becomes increasingly difficult to get out of your car or tie your shoes without getting out of breath, then some modifications or Photoshopping your image may be in store.

If your effectiveness is not up to your usual performance and you find yourself getting more and more intolerant and frustrated, it's time to take a look at what you're doing and either make some modifications or change your photo image to a completely different image . . . such as finding different ways to find happiness and enjoy life.

Some people may not have the advantage of self-employment and have retired, or have been forced into retirement from their jobs. Then there are those who willingly decided to retire and take the time to enjoy life with the intent of traveling, spending time with family, recreating, etc. Even with the best of intentions, many of these retirement plans fail to come to fruition due to any number of things that life has to throw at us in the form of other family needs, insufficient finances, and deteriorating health problems. These things can happen whether you're self-employed or not. Just because we may retire doesn't mean that regular life's issues cease to greet us when we least expect them.

Poor planning and poor choices are the number one cause of insufficient funds for one to enjoy retirement. There are those who spent money they didn't have on things they didn't need in order to impress people who couldn't care less. Then there are those who experienced medical expenses that wiped out whatever savings they had; lost their homes in fires, floods, or tornados/hurricanes and had insufficient insurance coverage. Perhaps the greatest contributing factor for unhappy retirement is not having saved early enough in life to afford to retire later in life. As the saying goes, "I started out with nothing and I have most of it left."

If you are a single person and find yourself in such conditions, this is when men shop for a nurse with a purse and women look for a financial provider. If married or in a committed relationship, then one or both of your finances when combined may (or may not) be sufficient for a somewhat comfortable or perhaps a very comfortable retirement.

For those who plan to work until they die, the real bugaboo is when they have to face reality that they are not as capable or efficient in their work as they have been in the past. Medical, physical, and memory problems can affect one's ability to be effective on the job. If so, then frustration may begin to enter the picture and emotional stress and intolerance may develop. The first inclination is to deny these factors are occurring and to see them as only temporary conditions that will soon improve. The reality is, more often than not, they become worse.

If you find yourself being continually frustrated more than usual it is time to look at your situation to determine whether or not it is time to say "When" and either slow down considerably in your work or retire altogether. Frustration and stress are not contributors to happiness. In fact, they can, and will, shorten your life by affecting your mental and physical health.

Life is a gift of which you have been given each day you wake up. Now, more than ever, take the time to enjoy it. If affordable, do those things you always wanted to do but haven't. If not affordable, discover other things that will bring you pleasure and happiness. So many people have gone to their grave feeling miserable. Looking back over your lifespan, is that how you want to go out?

We work hard for our money and money is meant to be spent not hoarded. It won't do you any good when your life is over. One man stipulated that when he died, he wanted to be buried in his Cadillac. When he died and the Cadillac was being put in the ground a person was heard to say, "Man, that's livin'."

Dealing With Your Own Mortality

I can no more advise you on effectively facing your own last days than I can cure you of your eventual cause of death. We are all different and we all have different perceptions and beliefs when it comes to death. What I can do, however, is suggest that you prepare for it before it happens.

When putting on undergarments, slacks, shorts, or pants, sit on the edge of your bed to don them. You aren't as able to maintain your balance as you once were. Many an elderly person has fallen and hit their head on a piece of furniture while getting dressed.

If you live alone, it may be wise for you to acquire a medical alert system. There are several to choose from and Medicare may cover some of them.

Have a will
Create a living trust as well to avoid probate.
Have all of your wishes spelled out as to how you wish to be buried or cremated and your material items divided and to whom. Most likely, you will have family

or friends who will have many things to do on your behalf when you die.

Have one place for all of your important documents;

- Insurance policies
- Investment accounts
- Bank accounts
- Military DD 214 if you served in the military.
- Credit Card numbers
- Social security #
- Will & Testament, and Living Trust
- Cemetery burial site docs if pre-purchased
- Medicare account info

I have yet to ever witness a Brinks armored vehicle ascend to heaven so make sure you specifically state how you wish your finances and other assets to be dispersed. Nothing leads to anger and resentment in families like disagreements over one's assets. Expectations that never occur, jealousy, and other resentment can rise even in the closest of families.

There is the story of a man who disclosed in his will that all of his money was to be buried with him when he died. His wife was named executor of his Last Will and Testament and had power of attorney to withdraw from any and all of his financial accounts upon his death.

When he died, she had all of his money transferred to her personal account and then she wrote a check for all of it and placed it in his casket just before burial. At least she followed her husband's wishes.

Action Item

If what you want is to feel better, live a long and happy, healthy life . . . what are the things you are doing to reach those goals? Take a serious look at your day-to-day behavior. How much of the things you do each day will help you feel better, live longer, be happy, and be healthy? What are the things you are doing that will keep you from reaching those goals? What are the things you could do if you only just took the first step?

Here are two things that everyone can do when dealing with those disturbing, depressing, anxiety-producing and anger-causing external pictures that lead to unhappiness, regardless of the situation.

1. **CHANGE WHAT YOU WANT.**

   You want to stay young and not grow older. Since you can't control the aging process, stop wanting to be something you can't control.

2. **CHANGE HOW YOU BEHAVE WHEN YOU DON'T GET WHAT YOU WANT.**

   Once you stop fighting the inevitable aging process and accept it, your thoughts and behaviors will lead to happier and more pleasant choices. As I said earlier, you can choose to be bitter or you can choose to be better. It's always a choice.

You can't control the weather, or the past, or growing older, or living forever, but you can control your thinking and your behavior. Either one, or both, will have the effect of controlling your emotions as well as your physiology. It is a choice of either changing what you want and/or changing how you choose to behave when you don't get what you want. It's just that simple and they are extremely easy choices to make.

One last pearl of wisdom to ensure happiness and serenity in your life comes from Dr. William Glasser, which I have modified from his global concept to an individual concept:

"If everyone would realize that what is right for them is not right for everybody, their life would be peaceful and happy."

In the end, it doesn't matter how much material things you may own, or what you may have accomplished in this life. That will all be forgotten after you're gone. All that will really matter is how you treated others that will earn you love and respect.

"And in the end, the love you take, is equal to the love, you make."

Paul McCartney

About the Author

 Mike Rice is certified in Reality Therapy and Choice Theory. He has lectured in Arizona at the AZ Psychological Association in Tempe, AZ; the Wm. Glasser West Region Conferences in Los Angeles; Loyola Marymount University, The Sierra Coast Council on Alcoholism and Drug Dependence in Sacramento, CA., and led a workshop at the Wm Glasser International Conference in Nashville, TN., and Las Vegas, NV. He Co-MC'd the opening ceremonies of the first William Glasser International Conference at Loyola Marymount University in Los Angeles, CA in June of 2012 as well as conducting a workshop at the event.

Mike is the CEO, Director, and Counselor for Court Counseling Services, Inc in Mesa, AZ and has been in private practice since 1998. Mike is currently the President of the West Region of the William Glasser Institute of the States of AZ, CA, NM, NV, and HI. He is also a current member of the William Glasser Institute-US Board or Directors.

References

Mike Rice

www.Mike-Rice.com

https://www.facebook.com/michael.rice.3557

https://www.facebook.com/pages/Court-Counseling-Services-Inc/144584812219942

William Glasser

www.WGlasser.com

www.wgiwestregion.com

https://www.facebook.com/pages/Glasser-West-Region/144022415712644

Mental Health

http://mentalhealthandhappiness.com/

www.therelationshipcenter.biz